wire
style2

wire
style 2
45 new jewelry designs

Denise Peck

INTERWEAVE
interweave.com

Editor	Anne Merrow
Technical Editor	Bonnie Brooks
Cover & Interior Design	Julia Boyles
Art Director	Liz Quan
Project Photography	Joe Coca
Step-by-step and Tools Photography	James Lawson
Video Studio Manager	Garrett Evans
Video Producer	Rachel Link
Production Design	Katherine Jackson

Interweave Press LLC
201 East Fourth Street
Loveland, CO 80537-5655 USA
interweave.com

Printed in China by Asia Pacific Offset Ltd.

Library of Congress Cataloging-in-Publication Data

Peck, Denise.
  Wire style 2 : 45 New Jewelry designs / by Denise Peck.
       p. cm.
  Includes index.
  ISBN 978-1-59668-255-9
  1. Jewelry making. 2. Wire jewelry. I. Title. II. Title: Wire style two.
  TT212.P426 2010
  739.27--dc22
                                    2010027406

10 9 8 7 6 5 4 3 2 1

dedication

For Paul, whose patience, encouragement, and love keep me steady.

contents

Projects

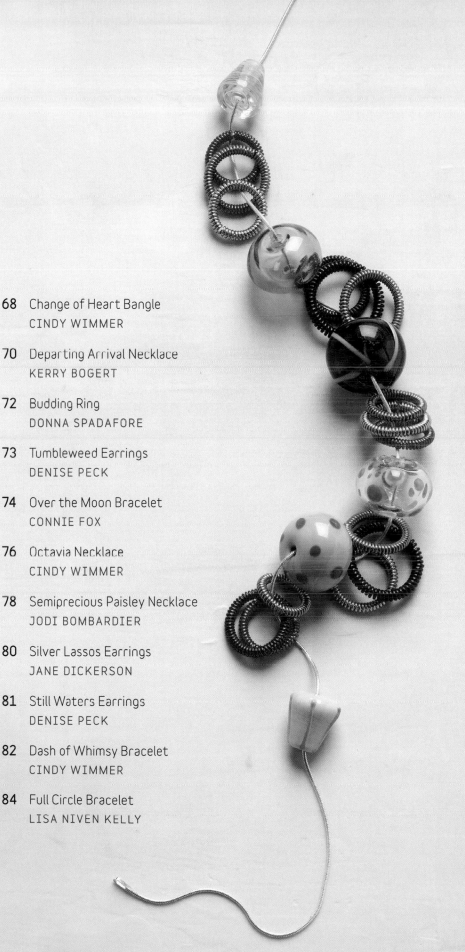

wrapped up
in wire

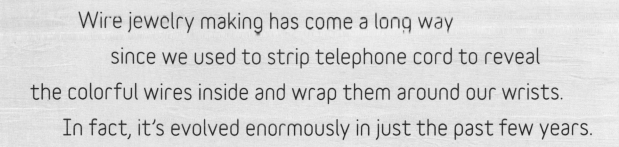

Wire jewelry making has come a long way
since we used to strip telephone cord to reveal
the colorful wires inside and wrap them around our wrists.
In fact, it's evolved enormously in just the past few years.

There are now defined genres of wirework, and artists are working in everything from sterling and gold to bronze, aluminum, and even rebar wire from the hardware store.

The versatility of wire makes it an ideal medium to work with in jewelry. Very fine wire can produce delicate, elegant designs, and the soft malleability of fine-gauge wire makes it very easy to work with. Sometimes the finest wire can take a backseat to the starring stones and invisibly showcase delicately faceted, sparkling gems. Heavier gauge wire can be hammered, textured, oxidized, and colorized and can result in dramatic, funky, chunky, statement pieces—true one-of-a-kind masterpieces. In fact, when you hammer heavier gauge wire, the result can look more like sheet metal than wire—a real trompe l'oeil.

Working with wire can be a stepping-stone from stringing to metalsmithing. You may find you want to expand your workbench tools. As wirework gets more sophisticated, the tools do, too. Though you can do almost anything with a set of pliers and a hammer, you'll find there's a world of tools that can make even the most tedious jobs quicker and easier, and produce better results. If any of the techniques are new to you (or for a refresher in wirework), check out the enclosed DVD for step-by-step instruction.

Wire Style 2 includes torch techniques and some designs that call for balling the ends of silver wire. You can easily begin with a small butane torch at your table for another transition into metalsmithing. When you can ball silver wire, you open up the possibility of making a whole array of your own jewelry findings. Personalize your designs even more by designing right down to the ear wires, head pins, and clasps. The sky's the limit. All you need is that jewelry-making bug—and I know you already have that. Enjoy!

wire basics

One of the best things about working with wire is that it's such a forgiving medium.

If you make a mistake, you can often restraighten the wire and begin again. Additionally, you can buy practice wire very inexpensively and create with impunity! Copper, brass, and colored craft wire are available in hardware and craft stores, and all of them can produce finished pieces every bit as beautiful as sterling silver and gold.

Wire comes in a large variety of metals, shapes, and sizes. The size or diameter of wire is known as the gauge. In the United States, the standard is Brown & Sharpe, also known as American Wire Gauge (AWG). The diameter of wire in inches or millimeters is translated into a numeral from 0 to 34, the higher the number, the thinner the wire. Most of the projects in this book use wire in 14-gauge through 24-gauge.

Wire also comes in a variety of shapes. You can buy round, half-round, and square wire. Round is most commonly used and easily available. Half-round has a flat side and is commonly used for ring shanks, and square wire has four flat sides. Both half-round and square wire must be ordered from a jeweler's supplier. In most cases, the choice of shape is purely aesthetic.

Additionally, a jeweler's supplier will offer wire in three hardnesses: dead soft, half hard, and full hard. Dead-soft wire is best if you're going to be manipulating it a lot because wire work-hardens as you work with it. Work-hardening stiffens the wire and makes it harder to bend. Eventually it can become so brittle that it can break with additional manipulation.

If you're weaving, coiling, or spiraling, you should work with dead-soft wire, as it's much easier on the hands. If you're making ear wires or not planning on working the wire too much, you can start with half-hard wire, which is already stiffer than dead-soft wire. There are no projects in this book that call for full-hard wire.

You can make jewelry out of both base-metal wire and precious-metal wire. The most common base-metal wire used in jewelry is copper, though aluminum, nickel silver, and brass are also available.

Sterling silver and gold are precious metals. The cost of gold wire is often prohibitive, so a common alternative is gold-filled wire, which is a base-metal wire covered with an outer layer of gold. Gold-filled wire is preferable to gold-plated wire because gold plating scratches and wears off easily.

As with the shape of the wire, the choice of metal is usually just a matter of personal preference. For more on different types of wire, see the enclosed DVD.

gauge	round	half-round	square
2g	●	◖	■
3g	●	◖	■
4g	●	◖	■
6g	●	◖	■
7g	●	◖	■
8g	●	◖	■
9g	●	◖	■
10g	●	◖	■
11g	●	◖	■
12g	●	◖	■
13g	●	◖	■
14g	●	◖	■
16g	●	◖	■
18g	•	◖	■
19g	•	◖	•
20g	•	◖	•
21g	•	-	•
22g	•	-	•
24g	·	-	·
26g	·	-	·

tools

Many wire jewelry projects require only two tools—pliers and cutters! Of course, there are plenty of supplemental tools to help simplify and enhance your work. Most wire workshops should have a set of good pliers and hammers, an anvil or steel bench block on which to hammer, some metal files for smoothing, and a supply of various-size mandrels around which you can coil wire. Mandrels can be anything from specialty tools for jewelry makers to pens and pencils, or even chopsticks.

Remember that tool prices reflect the quality of the tools you're buying and range from very inexpensive to very expensive. A good set of pliers will be the best investment you can make. A few of the projects inside call for a butane torch. As you advance in your wireworking skills, I know you'll yearn for a torch! They are available at most hardware stores and use butane fuel, the same fuel used in lighters.

General Tools

flush cutters

These are also called side cutters because the cut is made to the side. They have pointed, angled jaws that allow very close cuts in tight places. One side of the jaws is almost flat, the other is concave. Always hold the flat side of the cutters against your work and the concave side against the waste. The flat side creates a nice flush end on your work. Flush cutters are sold with a maximum gauge-cutting capacity; be sure to use cutters that can accommodate the wire you're using.

flush cutters

mandrels

A mandrel is a spindle, rod, or bar around which you can bend metal or wire. Mandrels come in a variety of shapes and sizes. Some are made specifically for bracelets, some for rings, and some for making bezels. Almost anything can be used as a mandrel to shape wire, including wooden dowels and other pieces of wire. A Sharpie marker is a good example—it's the perfect shape for making French ear wires.

Coiling Gizmo

When making a lot of small coils, this tool makes it a snap to coil many inches in a few minutes. Use a small C-clamp to anchor it to your table. It comes with two different-size coiling mandrels for small and larger diameter coils.

pin vise

Vises can hold a variety of tools, including blades and drill bits. They're perfectly suited for pinching and holding the end of a long piece of wire to enable you to turn smooth wire into twisted wire.

wire gauge

Also known as the Brown & Sharpe wire gauge, this tool looks a bit like a flat round gear (see page 17). It measures the diameter of your wire and is an essential tool for wire jewelry making.

butane torch

Small handheld torches are available in hardware stores and jewelry suppliers. They use butane and are filled from a canister like you would fill a cigarette lighter. Look for triple-refined butane, as regular lighter butane can cause an uneven flame in a torch. Use torches to make balled head pins and ear wires, which can be expensive to buy pre-made.

mandrels

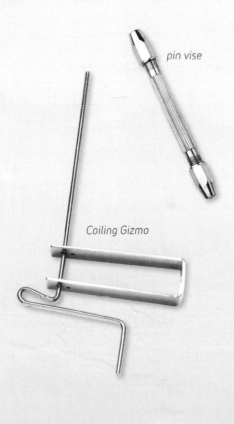

pin vise

Coiling Gizmo

butane torch

Pliers

bent-nose pliers

Also called bent chain-nose pliers, these are similar to chain-nose pliers (see below) but have a bend at the tip that allows access to tight places for tasks such as tightening coils and tucking in ends. Two pairs used together are also helpful for opening and closing jump rings.

chain-nose pliers

The workhorse of wire tools, chain-nose pliers are like needle-nose pliers but without teeth that can mar your wire. They are used for grasping wire, opening and closing jump rings, and making sharp angled bends. It's a good idea to have at least two pairs in your workshop for when you need one in each hand.

flat-nose pliers

Flat-nose pliers have broad, flat jaws and are good for making sharp bends in wire, grasping spirals, and holding components.

round-nose pliers

Another wireworker's necessity, round-nose pliers have pointed, graduated round jaws. They are used for making jump rings, simple loops, and curved bends in wire.

stepped forming pliers

Forming pliers come in different sizes and shapes. Stepped forming pliers have one chain-nose (or concave) jaw and one jaw of various-size round barrels. They're perfect for wrapping loops of consistent size.

wire-straightening pliers

These are also called nylon-jaw pliers because the jaws are made of hard nylon. Pulling wire through the clamped jaws will straighten any bends or kinks. They can also be used to hold, bend, or shape wire without marring the metal. Keep in mind that every time you pull wire through straightening pliers, you're work-hardening it, making it more brittle and harder to manipulate.

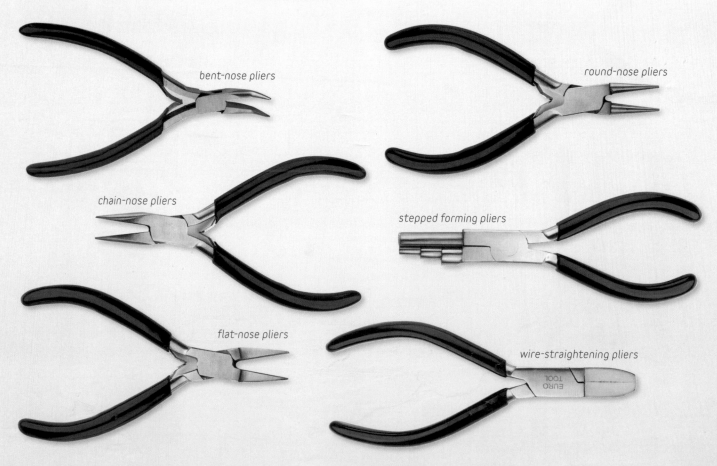

bent-nose pliers

round-nose pliers

chain-nose pliers

stepped forming pliers

flat-nose pliers

wire-straightening pliers

Hammering Tools

awls

awl

This common household tool comes in handy in a wire studio. A very sharp pointed tool, an awl usually has a wooden ball for a handle. Use it with a hammer to punch holes in flattened wire.

ball-peen hammer

Another staple in the studio, this hammer has one round domed head and one round flat head. The round head is used for making little dents for texture, while the flat head is used for flattening wire.

rawhide mallet

A hammer made of rawhide, this can be used on metal and wire without marring it. It's good for tapping wire into place or for hardening wire.

steel bench block

A bench block provides a small and portable hard surface on which to hammer wire. It's made of polished steel and is usually only ³/₄" (2 cm) thick and a few inches square. Use a bench block with a ball-peen hammer for flattening or texturing wire.

steel bench block

ball-peen hammer

rawhide mallet

Finishing Tools

liver of sulfur

Liver of sulfur is a chemical traditionally used to darken silver wire. It comes in a liquid or solid chunk form and is used for oxidizing, or antiquing, wire. When a small amount is mixed with hot water, it will turn a piece of wire dipped in it from blue to gray to black. Very fine steel wool can be used to finish oxidized silver.

needle files

Needle files are made for smoothing sharp ends of metal and wire. They're small and fine and come in different shapes for different purposes. A flat needle file is often all you need for smoothing wire ends.

polishing cloth

Jewelry polishing cloths are infused with a polishing compound and can be used for cleaning wire, eliminating tarnish, and hardening wire; pulling wire through the cloth repeatedly will stiffen, or work-harden, it. Pro Polish is one of the most popular brands.

rotary tumbler

Often associated with rock tumbling, this same electrical piece of equipment can be used to polish wire and metal jewelry.

liver of sulfur

needle files

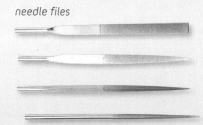

polishing cloth

rotary tumbler

wireworking techniques

As with tools, there are several basic techniques required to make wire jewelry. Over and above those, it's basically just tweaking a bit. If you can learn to make a nice round loop with your round-nose pliers, you're halfway there! Polishing and oxidizing can add a finishing touch.

The secret to fine wire jewelry is neatness. Ends should be neat and smooth or tucked out of sight. Coils should be tight and uniform, and loops should be round and centered. To see these techniques demonstrated and learn tips and tricks, see the enclosed DVD.

Basics

using a wire gauge

Brown & Sharpe or AWG (American Wire Gauge) is the standard in the United States for measuring the diameter of wire. When you use a wire gauge, use the small slots around the edge of the gauge, not the round holes at the ends of the slots. Place the wire edge into a slot **(figure 1)**. If there's wiggle room, place it into the next smaller slot. When you reach a slot that it will not fit into, then the number at the end of the next larger slot is the gauge of your wire.

flush cutting

Flush cutters have two sides, a flat side and a concave side. When you cut wire, you want the end that remains on your working piece to be flat, or flush. To do this, make sure the flat side of the cutters is facing your working piece when you snip.

straightening wire

Pulling a piece of wire through nylon-jaw pliers will straighten any bends in the wire. Grasp one end of the wire tightly in the nylon jaws and pull with your other hand **(figure 2)**. It may take two or three pulls through the pliers to straighten the wire completely. Be aware that the manipulation of wire in any pliers, including nylon-jaw pliers, will start the process of work-hardening the wire, which will eventually make it stiffer and harder to work with.

hammering

Always grasp the hammer firmly near the end of the handle. Do not "choke up" on the handle as you might a baseball bat. This assures you're using the weight of the head optimally and also keeps your hand from absorbing the shock of the impact.

piercing

If wire has been flattened, you can pierce it with an awl to make a hole for connecting other elements, such as ear wires. It's best to work on a scrap piece of wood. Take a sharp awl and position it where you want the hole. Push firmly to make an impression—a starter spot **(figure 3)**. Then place the point of the awl in the impression and strike the top sharply with a hammer **(figure 4)**.

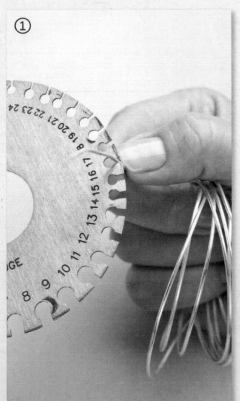

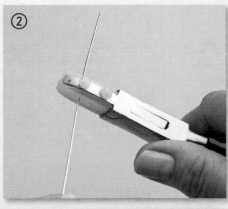

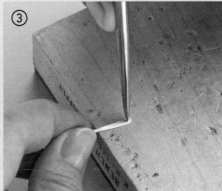

Torch Techniques

annealing

Annealing means heating wire or metal to a temperature where it becomes soft and malleable. When you work with any metal for a time, it will eventually become stiffer and harder to bend. That's called *work-hardened*. You can bring that malleability back with a torch. Run the flame back and forth several times along the length of wire you want to soften. (Wire is so thin that it doesn't need to glow in order to become annealed.) Use pliers to transfer it to a bowl of cold water to quench it before touching it.

balling

Hold one end of a length of copper, sterling, or fine silver wire with pliers or tweezers, and hold the other end perpendicular in the blue, hottest portion of the flame of the butane torch **(figure 1)**. When the wire balls up to the size you desire, remove it from the flame and quench it in a bowl of cool water. Copper and sterling will require that you remove the oxidation caused by the flame with a little steel wool.

Head Pins

balled head pin

Follow the instructions above to create a ball on one end of a 1"–3" (2.5–7.5 cm) length of wire.

flattened head pin

Hold 1"–3" (2.5–7.5 cm) length of any wire against a steel bench block and hammer $^1/_8$" (3 mm) flat with a ball-peen hammer **(figure 2)**.

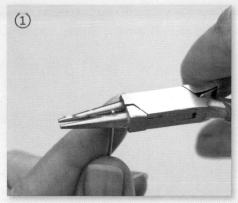

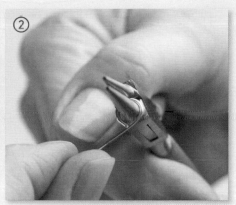

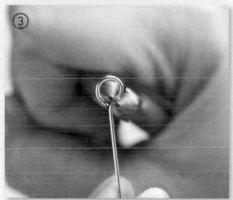

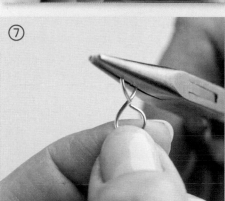

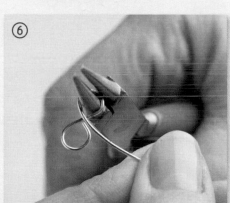

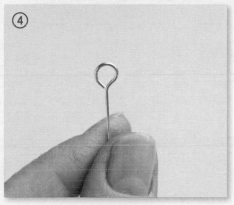

Loops

simple loops

Grasp the end of the wire in round-nose pliers so you can just see the tip of the wire **(figure 1)**. Rotate the pliers fully until you've made a complete loop **(figure 2)**. Remove the pliers. Reinsert the tip of the pliers to grasp the wire directly across from the opening of the loop. Make a sharp 45° bend across from the opening **(figure 3)**, centering the loop over the length of the wire like a lollipop **(figure 4)**.

figure-eight links

Make a loop on one end of the wire with round-nose pliers **(figure 5)**. Remove the pliers and grasp the wire just below the loop you just made. Pull the wire around the jaw of the pliers in the opposite direction of the first loop **(figure 6)**. Make sure you work at the same point on the jaw that you used to make the first loop so that the loops are the same size. Flush cut the end. *Optional:* Hold one loop with your fingers, grasp the other loop with chain-nose pliers, and twist a quarter turn so that the loops sit perpendicular to each other **(figure 7)**.

Loops (continued)

wrapped loops

Grasp the wire about 2" (5 cm) from the end with chain-nose pliers. Using your fingers, bend the wire flat against the pliers to 90° **(figure 1)**. With round-nose pliers, grasp the wire right at the bend you just made, holding the pliers perpendicular to the tabletop. Pull the wire up and over the top of the round-nose pliers **(figure 2)**. Pull the pliers out and put the lower jaw back into the loop you just made **(figure 3)**. Continue pulling the wire around the bottom jaw of the pliers into a full round loop **(figure 4)**. With your fingers or chain-nose pliers, wrap the wire around the neck of the lower wire two or three times **(figures 5 and 6)**.

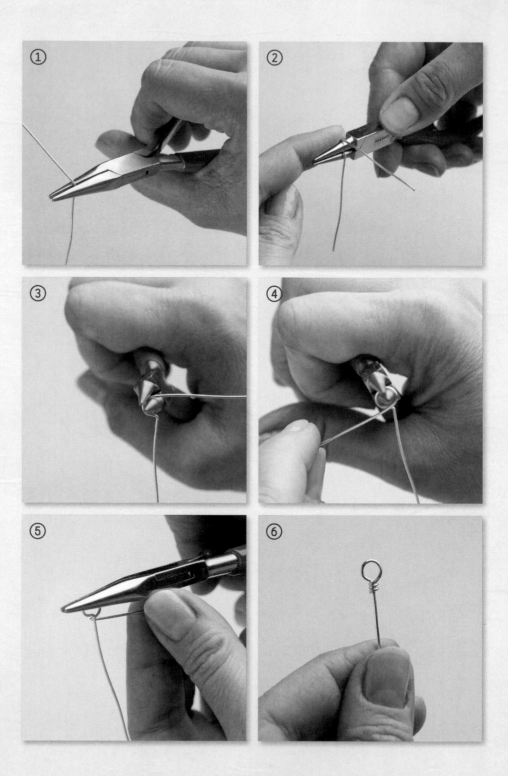

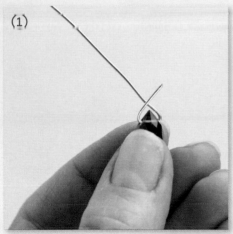
(1)

briolette loops

Briolette loops are commonly used for top-drilled stones. Insert a wire through the hole in a bead and bend up both sides so that they cross over the top of the bead **(figure 1)**. (You will only need a short length on one side.) Make a bend in each of the wires so they point straight up off the top of the bead. With flush cutters, trim the short wire so that it's no longer than 1/8" (3 mm) **(figure 2)**. Pinch the two wires together with chain-nose pliers and bend the longer wire over the top of the shorter wire to 90° **(figure 3)**. With round-nose pliers, make a wrapped loop by pulling the long wire up and over the round jaw **(figures 4 and 5)**. Wrap it around the neck of the two wires two or three times to secure **(figures 6 and 7)**.

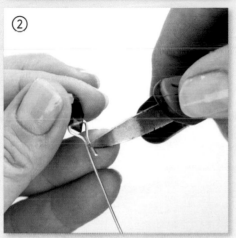
(2)

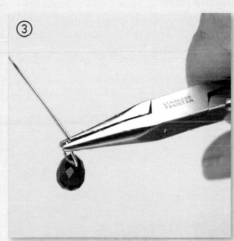
(3)

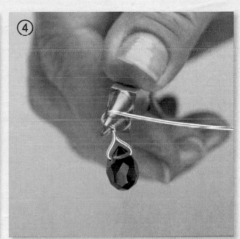
(4)

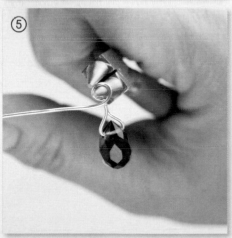
(5)

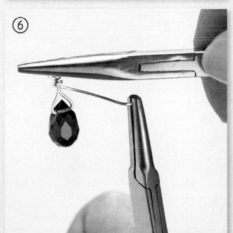
(6)

(7)

Coils and Spirals

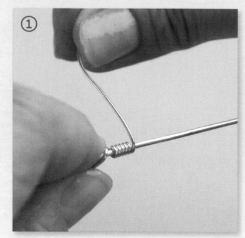

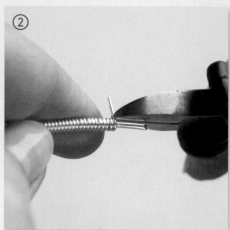

coiling

Coils can be made on any round mandrel, including another piece of wire. Hold one end of the wire tightly against the mandrel with your thumb and coil the length up the mandrel **(figure 1)**. Be sure to wrap snugly and keep the coils right next to one another. Flush cut both ends **(figure 2)**. Slide the coil off the mandrel.

spiraling

Make a very small loop with round-nose pliers **(figure 3)**. Grasp the loop in flat-nose pliers and use the thumb of your other hand to push the wire around the loop **(figure 4)**. Continue to move the spiral around in the jaws of the flat-nose pliers to enable you to enlarge the coil **(figure 5)**.

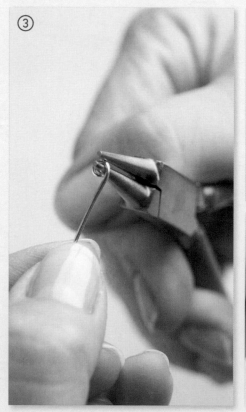

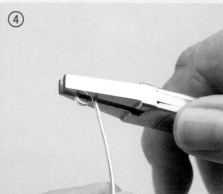

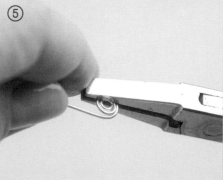

Jump Rings

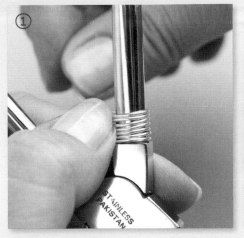

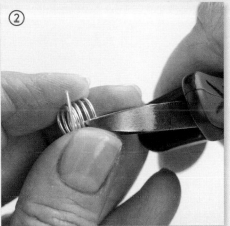

making jump rings

Coil wire snugly around a mandrel **(figure 1)**. Each single coil will make one jump ring. Remove the mandrel. Using flush cutters, cut through all the rings at the same spot along the length of the coil, snipping one or two at a time **(figure 2)**. They will fall away and each ring will be slightly open **(figure 3)**. The jump rings you make will have the inner diameter (ID) of the mandrel you used to make them.

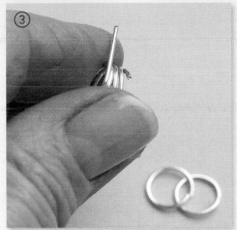

When purchasing jump rings, note that some vendors sell them by inner diameter measurements, and some vendors sell them by outer diameter measurements. The difference is minuscule and only essential if you're working on a complex chain maille design.

opening and closing jump rings

Always use two chain-nose or bent-nose pliers to open and close jump rings. Grasp the ring on each side of the opening with pliers **(figure 4)**. Gently push one side away from you while pulling the other side toward you, so the ring opens from side to side **(figure 5)**. To close, reverse the directions of your hands.

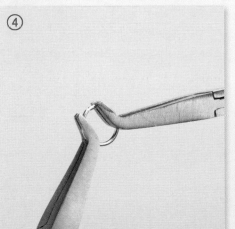

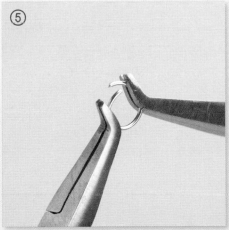

Hooks

simple hooks

Make a simple loop on the end of the wire with round-nose pliers. Hold a Sharpie marker against the wire above the loop and bend the wire over the marker and down parallel to the loop **(figure 1)**. Flush cut the long wire across from the loop. With round-nose pliers, make a small bend outward at the end of the hook **(figure 2)**. Flatten the curve of the hook with a ball-peen hammer to work-harden and strengthen the hook **(figures 3 and 4)**.

S-hooks

This clasp can be made in any size, depending on the length of wire you start with. With round-nose pliers, make a small loop on each end, going in opposite directions **(figure 5)**. Grasp one side with round-nose pliers just above the loop and bend the wire back over the pliers away from the loop **(figure 6)**. Turn the wire over and repeat in the opposite direction on the other end **(figure 7)**.

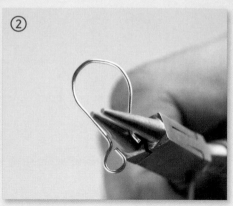

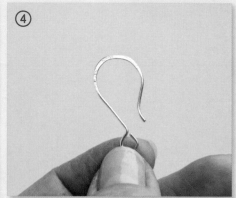

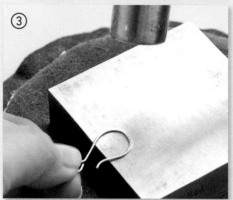

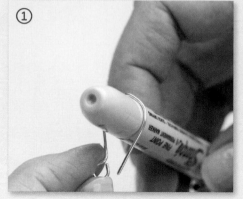

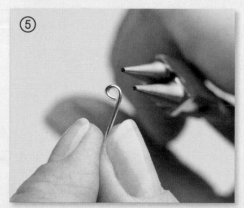

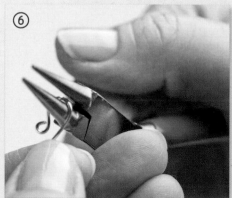

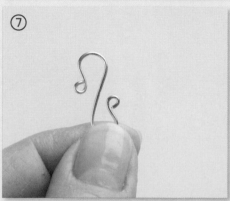

①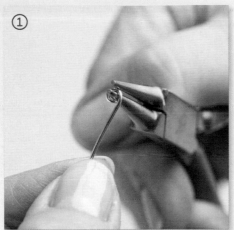

spiral hooks

This clasp can be made with a tight spiral or a loose, open spiral. Both begin with a small loop made with round-nose pliers **(figure 1)**. With flat-nose or nylon-jaw pliers, make a spiral **(figure 2)**. Leave about 2" (5 cm) of wire beyond the spiral and at the other end of the wire, flatten ¼" (6 mm) with a ball-peen hammer **(figure 3)**. Make a very small loop in the same direction as the spiral **(figure 4)**. Using pliers or your fingers, bend the length back away from the small loop and into a hook **(figure 5)**. Flatten the curve of the hook with a ball-peen hammer to work-harden and strengthen the hook **(figures 6 and 7)**.

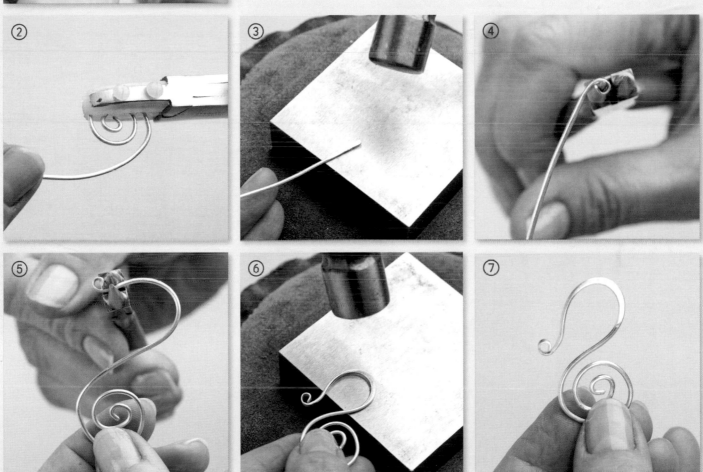

Ear Wires

basic ear wires

With round-nose pliers, make a small loop on the end of a 1¹/₂" (3.8 cm) length of wire **(figure 1)**. Hold the loop against a Sharpie marker and bend the wire over the marker away from the loop **(figure 2)**. With round-nose pliers, make a small bend outward at the end of the wire **(figure 3)**.

balled ear wires

Ball up the end (see page 18) of 1³/₄" (4.4 cm) of sterling, copper, or fine silver wire and quench in water to cool **(figure 4)**. Use round-nose pliers to make a small loop at the balled end **(figure 5)**. Hold the loop against a Sharpie marker and bend the wire over the marker away from the loop **(figure 6)**.

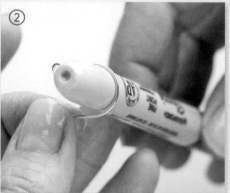

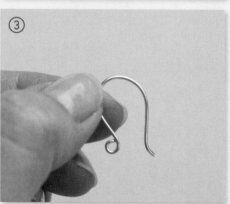

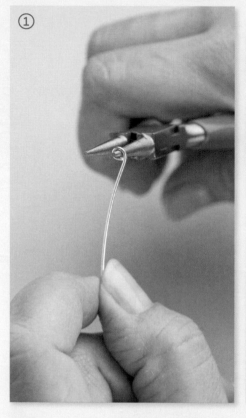

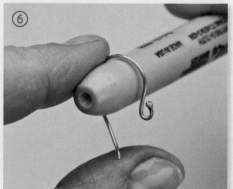

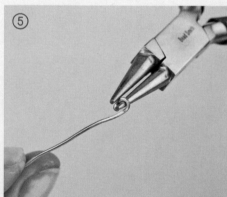

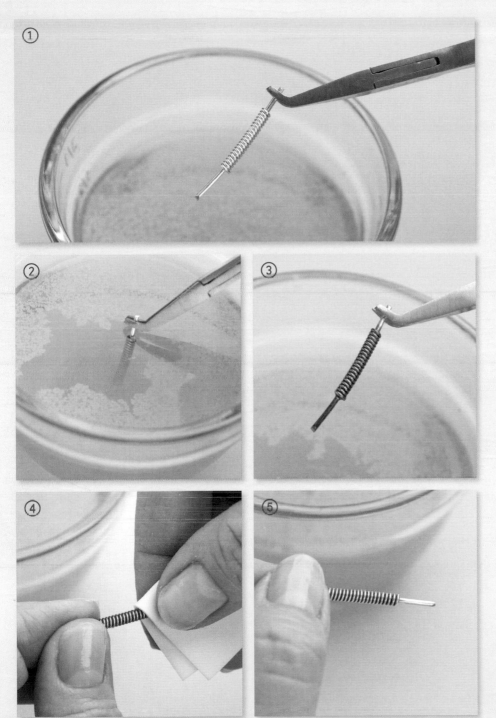

Finishing

oxidizing

Liver of sulfur is used to darken, or patina, wire. Dissolve a small lump of liver of sulfur in very hot water. Dip your piece into the solution **(figures 1 and 2)**. Depending on the temperature of the solution and the length of time you leave the piece in it, the wire can turn a variety of colors, including gold, blue, and black. Remove the piece when it reaches the desired color **(figure 3)**. Dry and polish it lightly to remove some of the patina **(figure 4)** but leave the dark color in the recesses of the piece **(figure 5)**.

tumbling

The barrel of a rotary tumbler must be filled with a tumbling medium such as stainless steel shot (available from jeweler's suppliers) and water. The tumbling action against the shot polishes the metal or wire to a high shine. The tumbling action also helps work-harden, or stiffen, the wire.

projects

Large hammered wrapped loops attached together draw your eye up and around this colorful necklace. Change up the color combinations for a different outcome.

Loopty Loo Necklace

DESIGNED BY **Lorelei Eurto**

1. Attach one end of each of the 4 brass chain sections to one end of the ceramic flower connector by opening the chain links with chain-nose and flat-nose pliers.

2. Attach one 7mm jump ring through all four ends of chain.

3. Create a toggle bar with a 1½" (3.8 cm) section of 20g wire as follows: Form a loop around the round-nose pliers in the middle of the wire so that one end points to the left and one end points to the right, forming a T shape. Hammer the ends of the wire flat and hammer the loop flat. Attach the loop to the 7mm jump ring at the end of the chain section.

4. Attach three 7mm jump rings to the other side of the ceramic flower connector.

5. Working with the length of brass wire, form a beaded link by making a large wrapped loop around the Sharpie marker. String 1 brass spacer, 1 ceramic round, 1 brass spacer. Form another wrapped loop and trim. Hammer each large loop flat with the ball-peen hammer. Add a little texture using the ball end of the hammer.

6. Attach the loop to the three 7mm jump rings at the top of the ceramic connector.

7. Repeat Step 5 with the remaining spacers and ceramic rounds. Attach each bead link to the previous link before wrapping closed.

8. Form the final loop around a smaller pen and attach this loop to the small hole in the ceramic leaf toggle.

LEVEL 1 ●

FINISHED SIZE: 21½" (54.5 cm)

TECHNIQUES USED
Opening and closing jump rings (23), hammering (17), wrapped loops (20)

materials

25" (63.5 cm) of oxidized brass 20-gauge wire
1 teal 40mm flower ceramic connector
1 green 25x40mm ceramic leaf toggle
6 ceramic 18mm rounds
12 brass 3mm spacers
4 brass 7mm jump rings
4 ½" (11.5 cm) oxidized brass 10mm round-link chain
4 ½" (11.5 cm) oxidized brass 5.2 x 7.2mm flat-oval chain
4 ½" (11.5 cm) etched oxidized brass 6.5 x 9.5 cable chain
4 ½" (11.5 cm) oxidized brass 3.5mm rolo chain

tools

Flat-nose pliers
Chain-nose pliers
Round-nose pliers
Large Sharpie marker
Ballpoint pen
Flush cutters
Ball-peen hammer
Steel bench block

resources

Ceramic flower connector: Chinook Jewelry. *Ceramic rounds:* Keith O'Connor. *Ceramic leaf toggle:* Every Heart Crafts. *Brass chain and jump rings:* Vintaj Brass Co. *Brass spacers:* Hands of the Hills. *Brass wire:* Patina Queen.

Do you have a special bead
tucked away waiting to be showcased?
Show off a treasured bead with
these continuous-looking wire links.

Encircled Bracelet

DESIGNED BY **Cindy Wimmer**

1 Cut the 16g wire into five 12" (30.5 cm) lengths. Place the 2mm mandrel at the center of one of the lengths and wrap 2½ coils in each direction. Repeat with the remaining 4 lengths of wire. Be sure that the wire tails are extended in opposite directions. Remove from the mandrel.

2 Bend both wire tails so that they are perpendicular and flush against the coils. Begin wrapping the top wire around the center coil counterclockwise. Then wrap both wires around in a circular direction, creating spirals that press against the center wires. Stop when there are 3 complete spirals around the center coil. The wire tails should be facing in opposite directions.

3 Trim the top wire to ¾" (2 cm) and make a simple loop on the side of the link that sits flush with the spirals. Trim the bottom wire to ¾" (2 cm) and bend it out to a 90° angle on the opposite side of the link. Make a simple loop that sits perpendicular to the link. Repeat Steps 1–3 to make 5 copper links.

4 Slide the lampworked bead onto the 16g wire and make simple loops on both ends.

5 Make a simple wire hook with the remaining 16g wire. Hammer the bend of the hook to flatten.

6 Open each of the loops on the wire links as you would jump rings. Attach the links together, ending with the lampworked focal on one end and the hook on the other.

7 Dip the bracelet in liver of sulfur solution and then buff with steel wool. Place in a rotary tumbler to work-harden and polish.

LEVEL 1

FINISHED SIZE: 8" (20.5 cm)

TECHNIQUES USED
Coiling (22), simple loops (19), hammering (17), simple hooks (24), opening and closing jump rings (23)

materials
5½' (1.7 m) of pure copper 16-gauge wire
1 lampworked 18x24mm focal bead

tools
Small round-nose pliers
Flat-nose pliers
Flush cutters
Ball-peen hammer
Steel bench block
2mm mandrel
Liver of sulfur
Fine steel wool, #0000
Rotary tumbler

resources
Lampworked bead: Jena Fulcher.

A sessile is a link, a permanent connection
    to be attached or fixed. It perfectly describes
        how these lampworked glass rings
            and wire components move together
throughout this lovely choker-length design.

Sessiled Necklace

DESIGNED BY **Kerry Bogert**

1. Cut two 9" (23 cm) pieces of 16g wire. With the 22g sterling wire, coil 8" (20.5 cm) of each 9" pieces. Flush cut the ends of the 22g wire.

2. Wrap the 16g coiled wire around the ½" mandrel. Slide this coil off the mandrel and cut it into coiled rings with wire cutters as though making jump rings. Use chain-nose pliers to bring the ring ends together and close the rings. Repeat to make 7 coiled ring links. Set aside.

3. Cut seven 6" (15 cm) pieces of 18g wire. Place the center of 1 piece against the ½" mandrel and wrap it around 1½ times so that several inches of wire extend straight out on either side of the newly formed ring. Gently open the ring just formed, slide on two lampworked glass rings, and close the wire ring.

4. With chain-nose pliers, grasp the 2 wires where they cross each other. Wrap one end around the ring wire as if to close a wrapped loop. Trim excess. Repeat this step with the second length of wire; the glass rings and wire ring are now connected.

5. Repeat Steps 3 and 4 to make seven 2-ring links, reserving 1 glass ring. Set aside.

6. With chain-nose pliers, open one of the coiled ring links created in Step 2. Add the reserved glass ring and a glass ring from one of the 2-ring links. Close the coiled ring link.

7. Continue building the necklace, joining the 2-ring links with the coiled ring links. Finish with a single coiled ring link on each end of the necklace.

8. With the remaining 16g sterling wire, make a simple hook. Add the hook to one of the end coiled ring links. The ring on the opposite end of the necklace will act as the catch for the hook.

LEVEL 1

FINISHED SIZE: 14½" (37 cm)

TECHNIQUES USED
Coiling (22), flush cutting (17), wrapped loops (20), making jump rings (23), simple hooks (24)

materials
20" (51 cm) of sterling silver 16-gauge dead-soft round wire

4' (1.2 m) of sterling silver 18-gauge dead-soft wire

1 oz spool of sterling silver 22g wire

3 lampworked glass ¾" (2 cm) rings

6 lampworked glass ⅝" (1.5 cm) rings

6 lampworked glass ½" (1.3 cm) rings

tools
Chain-nose pliers

Flush cutters

½" mandrel

resources
Lampworked glass beads: Kab's Creative Concepts.

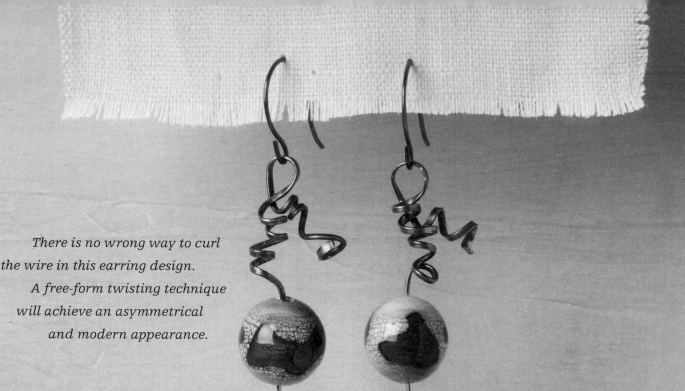

There is no wrong way to curl the wire in this earring design. A free-form twisting technique will achieve an asymmetrical and modern appearance.

Rustic Globes Earrings

DESIGNED BY **Lorelei Eurto**

1. Cut the wire in half.
2. Hammer ⅛" (3mm) of the end of one wire flat using the hammer and bench block. String the bead on the wire. Hammer the rest of the wire flat.
3. Curl the wire around the jaw of the round-nose pliers all the way down the wire from the end to the top of the bead. Make some of the loops smaller and some larger for added interest.
4. Make a simple loop 1" (2.5 cm) from the end of the wire. Bend the tail so that it sticks out to one side. Attach an ear wire to the simple loop.
5. Repeat Steps 2–4 for the second earring.

LEVEL 1 ●

FINISHED SIZE: 2¼" (5.5 cm)

TECHNIQUES USED
Hammering (17), simple loops (19)

materials
6" (12.5 cm) of oxidized brass 20-gauge wire
2 gold 15mm lampworked glass rounds
2 brass French ear wires

tools
Flush cutters
Round-nose pliers
Ball-peen hammer
Bench block

resources
Lampworked glass rounds: Gardanne Glass.
Earring wires: Vintaj Brass Co. *Brass wire:*
Patina Queen.

*Combining metals always adds
an element of surprise.
Switch it up by wrapping silver
with fine copper wire
or change the look completely
by using gold and silver.*

Copper Links Earrings

DESIGNED BY **Denise Peck**

1 Coil the 18g wire tightly around the pen. Cut the coil into 6 jump rings. File the ends flat.

2 Hammer all the jump rings to flatten.

3 Link 3 flattened jump rings together. Cut three 6" (15 cm) pieces of 26g wire and coil one tightly around the seam of each copper jump ring. Trim and pinch the ends flat with the chain-nose pliers. Add an ear wire to one end. Repeat for second earring.

4 Dip the earrings in liver of sulfur solution and then buff with steel wool. Place in a rotary tumbler to work-harden and polish.

LEVEL 1 ●

FINISHED SIZE: 2" (5 cm)

TECHNIQUES USED
Coiling (22), making jump rings (23), hammering (17), oxidizing (27)

materials
6" (15 cm) of copper 18-gauge wire
1' (30.5 cm) of sterling silver 26-gauge dead-soft wire
2 copper ear wires

tools
Chain-nose pliers
Flat-nose pliers
Flush cutters
Metal file
Round pen or pencil
Ball-peen hammer
Steel bench block
Liver of sulfur
Polishing cloth
Fine steel wool, #0000
Rotary tumbler

resources
Copper and silver wire: Metalliferous. *Ear wires:* Artbeads.

Finally, a fun version of a childhood game
that doesn't require perfect aim.
Clustered groupings of colorful coiled rings
play with equally colorful hollow-
formed lampworked glass beads.
The fresh, crisp color evokes warm summer days.

Ring Toss Necklace

DESGINED BY **Kerry Bogert**

1. Cut five 8" (20.3 cm) lengths of 16g sterling wire. Coil the orange-colored copper wire tightly around an 8" (20.5 cm) length of 16g sterling wire. Repeat for the remaining 4 colors of wire. Trim excess colored wire and set aside.

2. Coil one of the coil-covered pieces of 16g wire around the ½" (1.3 cm) mandrel. Remove the coil from the mandrel and cut the coil into rings (as if making jump rings on a larger scale). Use chain-nose pliers to line up the ring ends and close each ring.

3. Repeat Step 2 for the remaining colors, varying the size of the mandrel, to make 15 rings total. (If you don't have multiple sizes of mandrels, look around your studio for alternative objects that can be used as mandrels. Paintbrush handles, bottles of nail polish, permanent markers, or tubes of seed beads are just a few items that can be used as mandrels.)

4. String 1 cone bead, 3 coiled rings, 1 hollow bead, 3 coiled rings, 1 hollow bead, 3 coiled rings, 1 hollow bead, 3 coiled rings, 1 hollow bead, 3 coiled rings, and 1 cone bead onto the sterling silver snake chain.

LEVEL 1

FINISHED SIZE: 18" (46 cm)

TECHNIQUES USED
Coiling (22), making jump rings (23)

materials

4' (1.2 m) of 20-gauge colored copper wire in orange, turquoise, flag blue, green, and purple

40" (1 m) of sterling silver 16-gauge dead-soft round wire

4 brightly colored 20mm lampworked glass hollow beads

2 brightly colored 15mm lampworked glass cone beads

1 sterling silver 18" (45.5 cm) 1.5mm snake chain

tools

Chain-nose pliers
Flush cutters
1/2" mandrel
3/8" mandrel
3/4" mandrel

resources

Colored wire: Paramount Wire Co.
Lampworked beads: Kab's Creative Concepts.
Snake chain: Rio Grande.

*The scrolling wire accents
in this bracelet design
dress up what would otherwise be
ordinary beach stones.
Keeping the stones consistent in size
will help create a cohesive look.*

Scrolling Stones Bracelet

DESIGNED BY **Lorelei Eurto**

1 Cut five 1" (2.5 cm) pieces of brass wire. Use the round-nose pliers to create an S shape with each wire piece, curling one end up and the other end down. Hammer each link flat using the hammer and bench block. Repeat with all 5 pieces.

2 Cut four 1¼" (3.2 cm) pieces of brass wire. Create scroll links as follows: Make a cursive L shape with each wire. Curl the wire ends in toward the center of the L shape. Hammer each link flat.

3 Create a spiral hook for the clasp with a 1½" (3.8 cm) section of wire by forming a simple loop on one end. At the other end, use flat-nose pliers to create a loose spiral that can fit through the 10mm jump ring.

4 Attach a 7mm jump ring to the 10mm jump ring. Attach 1 stone and 1 S from Step 1 to the 7mm jump ring. Attach another 7mm jump ring to the other hole in the stone and the S so that the S lies flat across the top of the stone. Before closing the jump ring, attach a scroll link.

5 Repeat Step 4 to join the remaining stones and wire links. At the end of the bracelet, use a 7mm jump ring to attach the spiral hook.

LEVEL 1

FINISHED SIZE: 8" (20.5 cm)

TECHNIQUES USED
Hammering (17), simple loops (19), spiraling (22), opening and closing jump rings (23)

materials
13" (33 cm) of oxidized brass 20-gauge wire
10 brass 7mm jump rings
1 brass 10mm jump ring
5 double-drilled 18mm river stones

tools
Round-nose pliers
Flat-nose pliers
Flush cutters
Ball-peen hammer
Steel bench block

resources
Brass wire: Patina Queen. *Drilled stones:* Stones Studios Inc. *Jump rings* Vintaj Brass Co.

What do you do with those extra pieces
of coil saved from previous projects?
Turn your coil bits into a graduated pendant,
just like a coil quilt!

Quilted Coil Necklace

DESIGNED BY **Cindy Wimmer**

1 Coil the entire lengths of 22g twisted wire, 22g wire, 20g wire, and 18g wire on the 2mm mandrel. Remove from mandrel.

2 Flush cut a 9" (23 cm) piece of 14g wire. Hammer the tip of the wire, then create a small loop on the end with round-nose pliers. Create a spiral by holding the loop with flat-nose pliers and rotate for 2 turns. Hammer this spiral.

3 With flat-nose pliers, continue to turn the wire around the hammered spiral to create a loose spiral. Continue building the spiral, keeping the wire close but not touching. Leave a 1" (2.5 mm) tail.

4 Cut pieces varying in length from each of the wire coils for a total of 6" (15 cm) of coil pieces. Slide the coil pieces onto the loose spiral, pushing them as tightly as possible toward the center.

5 After the last coil piece has slid into place, trim the wire tail to 7/8" (2.2 cm). Using the back of the large round-nose pliers, create a simple loop. Using the flat-nose pliers, turn the loop perpendicular to the spiral. Reinsert the large round-nose pliers and roll upward, centering the loop over the spiral.

6 Medium spiral: Flush cut a 7½" (19 cm) piece of 14g wire. Repeat Steps 2–5, this time adding 4½" (11.5 cm) of coiled pieces.

7 Small spiral: Flush cut a 6½" (16.5 cm) piece of 14g wire. Repeat Steps 2–5, this time adding 3½" (9 cm) of coiled pieces.

8 Cut a 1½" (3.8 cm) piece of 14g wire and create a figure-eight link. Repeat to make a second link. Attach one to each end of the 26" (66 cm) chain. Cut a 5" (12.5 cm) piece of 14g wire and make a spiral hook. Attach the hook to one of the figure-eight links.

9 Open the loop of the large spiral as you would a jump ring and attach it to the medium spiral. Open the loop of the medium spiral and attach it to the small spiral. Attach the small spiral to the chain.

10 Dip the necklace in a liver of sulfur solution and then buff with steel wool if desired. Place in a rotary tumbler to work-harden and polish.

LEVEL 2 ● ●

FINISHED SIZE: 28" (71 cm)

TECHNIQUES USED
Coiling (22), flush cutting (17), hammering (17), simple loops (19), spiraling (22), figure-eight links (19), spiral hooks (25), opening and closing jump rings (23)

materials

5' (1.5 m) of sterling silver 22-gauge twisted wire

3' (.9 m) of sterling silver 14-gauge dead-soft wire

3' (.9 m) of sterling silver 18-gauge dead-soft wire

3' (.9 m) of sterling silver 20-gauge half-hard wire

3½' (1 m) of sterling silver 22-gauge half-hard wire

26" (66 cm) of sterling silver 4x6mm chain

tools

Large round-nose pliers
Small round-nose pliers
Flat-nose pliers
Flush cutters
2mm steel mandrel
Ball-peen hammer
Steel bench block
Liver of sulfur
Fine steel wool, #0000 (optional)
Polishing cloth
Rotary tumbler

resources
Twisted wire: Fundametals.

String large-hole beads
onto thick-gauge wire
in this bangle-style bracelet.
Use a different-shaped focal bead
as a design alternative.

Copper Coils Bracelet

DESIGNED BY **Lorelei Eurto**

1. Cut the copper wire into 3" (7.5 cm) lengths.

2. Create 4 copper-wire-coiled beads as follows: Wrap a 3" (7.5 cm) piece of 22g copper wire around one jaw of the round-nose pliers 10–12 times, making a ¼" (6mm) long bead. Repeat 3 more times and set aside.

3. With round-nose pliers, form a simple loop on the end of the 8" (20.5 cm) piece of 18g brass wire. Form the wire around your wrist or a bracelet mandrel into a bangle shape.

4. Attach a 10mm jump ring to each copper Mykonos bead. Attach a 7mm jump ring to each of the 10mm jump rings. Set them aside.

5. String 1 brass bead cap, 1 lampworked spacer, 1 copper coil, 1 brass spacer, and 1 Mykonos bead charm from Step 4 onto the bangle wire.

6. String 1 lampworked spacer, 1 agate, 1 brass spacer, 1 wood round, 1 Mykonos bead charm, 1 brass spacer, 1 copper coil, 1 prehnite round, 1 copper seed bead onto the bangle wire. Continue stringing onto the bangle wire the lampworked glass focal coin bead, 1 copper seed bead, 1 copper coil, 1 Mykonos bead charm, 1 copper seed bead, 1 lampworked spacer, 1 brass spacer, 1 agate, 1 lampworked spacer, 1 copper seed bead, 1 Mykonos bead charm, 1 copper coil, 1 brass spacer, 1 wood round, 1 prehnite round, 1 brass spacer, 1 lampworked glass spacer, 1 brass bead cap.

7. Form a simple loop on the end of the 18g wire and trim any excess wire with flush cutters.

8. Form a spiral hook using the 22g brass wire. Turn the hook portion 90° with flat-nose pliers.

9. Attach a 7mm jump ring to each end of the bangle. Attach the hook to one of these jump rings.

LEVEL 1 ●

FINISHED SIZE: 8½" (21.5 cm)

TECHNIQUES USED

Coiling (22), simple loops (19), opening and closing jump rings (23), spiral hooks (25)

materials

8" (20.5 cm) of oxidized brass 18-gauge wire
2" (5 cm) of oxidized brass 20-gauge wire
12" (30.5 cm) of oxidized copper 22-gauge wire
6 brass 7mm jump rings
4 brass 10mm jump rings
4 copper metallic 15mm ceramic triangle Mykonos beads
1 lampworked glass 22mm focal coin bead
2 faceted prehnite 8mm rounds
5 lampworked glass 5mm spacers
4 copper size 6° metal seed beads
6 brass 3mm spacers
2 wood 10mm rounds
2 crazy lace agate smooth rondelles
2 brass 4mm bead caps

tools

Round-nose pliers
Flush cutters
2 pairs flat-nose pliers
Bracelet mandrel (optional)

resources

Lampworked focal: Gardanne Glass. *Lampworked spacers:* Studio Rent, Kelley's Beads. *Prehnite, agate, brass spacers, brass jump rings:* Fusion Beads. *Copper seed beads:* Bello Modo. *Brass bead caps:* Ornamentea. *Wood rounds:* E&E Bungalow. *Brass and copper wire:* Patina Queen. *Ceramic beads:* The Mykonos.

The fun texture and playful colors
of this large lampworked button
make you want to pinch its beady cheeks!
Keep the color going with vintage chain
and a nifty pair of neatly wrapped bails.

Cute as a Button Necklace

DESIGNED BY **Kerry Bogert**

1. Cut an 8" (20.5 cm) piece of silver wire. With round-nose pliers, form a U-shaped bend about 2" (5 cm) from one end. String the lampworked glass button onto the wire and let it settle in the bend. Coil the shorter length of wire around the longer length, trapping the glass button on the wire.

2. Using round-nose pliers, form a ¼" (6mm) wrapped loop with the longer length. Wrap over the existing wraps from Step 1 two times; do not trim the excess.

3. Coil an 18" (45.5 cm) piece of 20g orange-colored copper wire around the length of wire left on the wrapped loop, leaving about ½" (1.3 cm) of bare wire exposed. Trim the colored wire flush against the silver wire.

4. Grasp the bare wire with chain-nose pliers and wrap the colored coil-covered wire around the area just below the wire loop. Tuck the excess wire inside the wrapping.

5. Repeat Steps 1–4 on the other side of the button.

6. Using the 3mm mandrel or Gizmo, coil a 4' (1.2 m) piece of blue-colored copper wire to create a 4" (10 cm) coil of wire. Trim the ends and cut the coil in half.

7. With remaining silver wire, make a figure-eight link and simple hook.

8. Thread an 18" (45.5 cm) piece of vintage enameled chain through one loop on the button link. Add a 2" (5 cm) piece of blue-colored wire coil to one side of the chain. (These coils are designed to move and play, not stay in one spot.) Bring the ends of chain together and attach the hook.

9. Repeat Step 7 on the other side of the button link. Finish by adding the figure-eight link to the ends of the chain.

LEVEL 1

FINISHED SIZE: 22" (56 cm)

TECHNIQUES USED
Coiling (22), wrapped loops (20), figure-eight links (19), simple hooks (24)

materials
18" (45.5 cm) of sterling silver 18-gauge dead-soft wire

6' (1.8 m) of orange-colored copper 20-gauge wire

4' (1.2 m) of light blue-colored copper 20-gauge wire

3' (.9 m) of vintage enameled blue 1.5mm cable chain

1 orange 35mm lampworked glass button

tools
Chain-nose pliers
Round-nose pliers
Flush cutters
3mm mandrel or Coiling Gizmo

resources
Colored wire: Paramount Wire Co.
Lampworked glass button: Kab's Creative Concepts. *Vintage chain*: Etsy.

It's all about the drama of multiple strands
   on this piece. And though it may look complex,
it's made on easily malleable wire
      with a rainbow of seed beads.
   Much of the construction can be done with your fingers.

Quiet Spaces Necklace

DESIGNED BY **Jane Dickerson**

1 Cut 36" (91.5 cm) of 24g wire. String 1 seed bead in any color, allowing it to settle 3" (7.5 cm) from one end.

2 Holding the bead in place, fold the wire down on each side of the bead. Pinch both wires together tightly under the seed bead. Using chain-nose pliers, grasp the seed bead gently and twist it so that the pinched wires wrap once or twice around each other. Bring the wires back to horizontal.

3 String another seed bead the same color as in Step 1 onto the longer end and allow it to settle about 1" (2.5 cm) from the first. Repeat Step 2. Continue adding beads in this manner until the beaded portion of the wire is about 15" (38 cm) long. Set aside.

4 Repeat Steps 1–3 to make 8 more beaded wires, 1 in purple AB beads and 2 in each of the other colors (including the cube beads).

5 Gather one end of all 9 beaded wire strands together. Wrap 2 of the wires around the remaining 7 wires as close to the end beads as possible 2–3 times. Make sure the wraps are neat and tight, then trim the excess wire. Continue wrapping the wires 2 at a time around the previous wraps and trimming the excess wire. Wrap the final wire and trim the excess. Repeat this step for the other end of the necklace.

6 Cut 5" (12.5 cm) of 20g wire. Thread one end of the 20g wire through the middle of the bunch of beaded wires just below the wrapped portion on one end of the necklace. Create a wrapped loop small enough to be concealed in the end cone. String 1 end cone, make a wrapped loop, and trim the excess wire. Repeat this step for the other end of the necklace.

7 Attach one 10mm jump ring to the wrapped loop on one end of the necklace. Use a 5mm jump ring to attach the clasp to the other end of the necklace.

LEVEL 2

FINISHED SIZE: 16 1/2" (42 cm)

TECHNIQUES USED
Flush cutting (17), wrapped loops (20), opening and closing jump rings (23)

materials

27' (8.2 m) of copper 24-gauge wire

10" (25.5 cm) of copper 20-gauge wire

60–70 each of size 6° seed beads in purple, green, and copper

30–35 purple AB size 6° seed beads

30–35 green size 4° cube beads

2 torched copper 15x12.5mm end cones

1 copper 10mm jump ring

1 copper 5mm jump ring

1 copper 18mm lobster clasp

tools

Chain-nose pliers

Round-nose pliers

Flush cutters

resources

24-gauge copper wire: Hardware store. *20-gauge wire:* Metalliferous. *Matte copper seed beads:* York Beads. *All other beads:* Melek Karacan. *Torched end cones:* Silk Road Treasures. *Clasp and jump rings:* Bead Empire.

Dreaming in Sepia Necklace

DESIGNED BY **Cindy Wimmer**

You don't have to raid
your great-aunt's jewelry box
to create this vintage-looking necklace.
Combine steel wire with crystal
in this edgy piece.

1. Hook: Coil the 24g wire onto the 16g wire mandrel to make a 2½" (6.5 cm) long coil. Measure a 1" (2.5 cm) piece of coil and cut, setting the remaining 1½" (3.8 cm) aside. Cut a 4" (10 cm) piece of 19g wire. With the round-nose pliers, create a small simple loop at the end of the wire, slide on the coil, and make a wrapped loop with the remaining wire. Measure ½" (1.3 cm) from the end of the simple loop and bend the coil over the back of the round-nose pliers to create a hook.

2. Centerpiece: Cut 10" (25.5 cm) of 19g wire. Measure 3" (7.5 cm) from the end of the wire and make a wrapped loop, using the back of the round-nose pliers to create a large loop. Wrap the tail around 3 times, then hammer the loop. String a crystal rondelle. Make a wrapped loop above the rondelle, using the widest portion of a Sharpie pen for the loop. Before completing the loop, slide on the 1½" (3.8 cm) coil. Wrap the tail 3 times.

3. Dangles: Cut 3 pieces of chain as follows: 9 links, 11 links, and 12 links. Make a wrapped-loop eye pin by beginning a wrapped loop at each end of a 2" (5 cm) piece of 24g wire. Add all 3 chain lengths before closing a wrapped loop at one end. Attach the eye pin to the plain loop on the coiled center piece with a wrapped loop at the other end of the wire. Wrap until all the wire is used. Cut two 5" (12.5 cm) pieces of 24g wire and make them into head pins by making a small simple loop at one end of each wire. Add the pearl to one and a Cosmic crystal and crystal rondelle to the other. Attach them with wrapped loops next to the dangling pieces of chain, continuing to wrap until all the wire is used.

4. Make a 2" (5 cm) head pin with 24g wire, add the bicone, and make a small wrapped loop with the tip of the round-nose pliers. Continue to wind over the wraps until all of the wire is used. Set aside.

5. Cut two 7½" (19 cm) pieces of chain. Cut an 8" (20.5 cm) piece of 22g wire. Make a wrapped loop at one end of the wire using the back of the round-nose pliers, attaching it to the centerpiece. Wrap the tail wire around 3 times and trim. Make a second loop, this time adding the 2 pieces of chain just cut. Close the loop and wrap the tail over the previous wraps to create a chunky wrapped link.

6. At the other end of the chains, add 3 more chunky wrapped links (as in Step 5) to create an extender chain. Attach the bicone charm from Step 4 to the end link.

7. Cut two 8¼" (21 cm) pieces of chain. Cut 12" (30.5 cm) of 22g wire. Make a wrapped loop 4" (10 cm) from the end of the wire and attach to the coiled centerpiece. Wrap the tail around 3 times, then wrap again 3 times over the first 3. Add 1 rondelle, 1 Cosmic crystal, and 1 rondelle. Make a wrapped loop to attach the link to the 2 pieces of chain. Complete the wrapped loop by wrapping 2 more times.

8. Make a chunky wrapped link with 22g wire as in Step 5 and attach it to the hook. Before closing the loop, attach 2 pieces of chain.

9. Using fine-grit sandpaper, sand all of the steel wire components.

LEVEL 1 ●

FINISHED SIZE: 20" (51 cm)

TECHNIQUES USED
Coiling (22), simple loops (19), wrapped loops (20), simple hooks (24), hammering (17)

materials

6" (15 cm) of black 19-gauge annealed steel wire

4 1/2' (1.4 m) of black 22-gauge annealed steel wire

4 1/2' (1.4 m) of black 24-gauge annealed steel wire

3' (.9 m) of antique silver-plated steel chain with 2x2mm links

2 silver 12mm Swarovski Cosmic crystals

1 silver 4mm Swarovski bicone crystal

4 clear 6mm Swarovski crystal rhinestone rondelles with black metal

1 bronze-colored 7mm pearl

tools

16-gauge piece of copper wire mandrel for coiling

Sharpie fine-tip marker

Small round-nose pliers

Chain nose-pliers

Flat nose-pliers

Flush cutters

Ball-peen hammer

Steel bench block

Fine-grit sandpaper

resources

Chain: Original Findings. *Swarovski crystal rondelles:* Walter's Beads. *Swarovski Cosmic crystals:* Artbeads. *Steel wire:* Ace Hardware or local hardware store.

The versatility of creating your own earring wires allows you to experiment with any metals. Try an alternative metal such as brass for a whole new look.

Odds or Evens Earrings

DESIGNED BY **Lorelei Eurto**

1. Cut the wire in half.
2. At 2" (5 cm) from one end of one wire, bend the wire over the Sharpie marker, forming a U shape.
3. At 1" (1.3 cm) from the longer end of the wire, form a wrapped loop, then trim excess wire with the flush cutters. String 1 lampworked glass ring and 1 copper number charm.
4. At 1" (1.3 cm) from the shorter end of the wire, bend the wire to a 90° angle so that the wire points to the wrapped loop.
5. Bend the wire up ¼" (6 mm) from the end of the wire. This end will slip into the loop and anchor it firmly.
6. Repeat Steps 2–5 for the second earring.
7. File the ends of the ear wires smooth.

LEVEL 1 ●

FINISHED SIZE: 2" (5 cm)

TECHNIQUES USED
Wrapped loops (20)

materials

11" (28 cm) of sterling silver 20-gauge
   half-hard wire
2 lampworked glass 1" (2.5 cm) rings
2 copper ½" (1.3 cm) number charms

tools

Flush cutters
Round-nose pliers
Chain-nose pliers
Flat-nose pliers
Metal file
Large Sharpie marker

resources

Lampworked glass rings: Kab's Creative
Concepts. *Copper number charms:* Zoa Art.
Silver Wire: EmMi Beads.

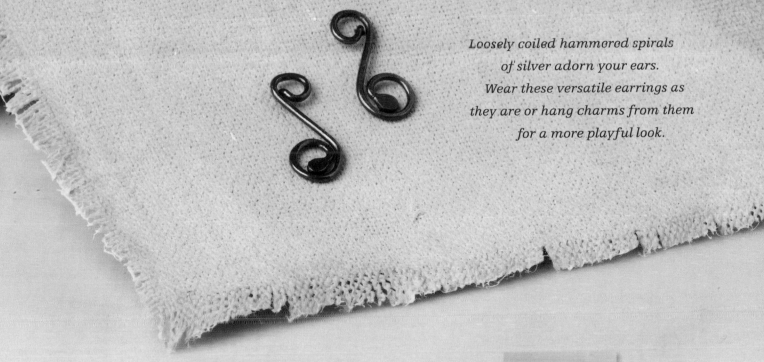

*Loosely coiled hammered spirals
of silver adorn your ears.
Wear these versatile earrings as
they are or hang charms from them
for a more playful look.*

Double Spiral Earrings

DESIGNED BY **Donna Spadafore**

1. Ball one end of each piece of wire using a torch.
2. Cut the wire 2" (5 cm) from the end of the ball. File the end smooth; this will be the earring post.
3. Bend the wire 90° with the flat-nose pliers ³⁄₈" (1 cm) from the un-balled end of each wire.
4. Holding the wire at the bend, wrap with round-nose pliers as if starting a spiral. Create a simple loop with the bent portion of the wire meeting the straight portion of the wire.
5. Grasp the other end of the wire with round-nose pliers just behind the ball and make a small spiral with an open center.
6. Adjust the top and bottom spirals until they look equal in size.
7. Repeat Steps 2–6 for second earring, making the spirals in the opposite direction from the first earring.
8. Dip the earrings in liver of sulfur solution. Do not buff or polish.

LEVEL 1 ●

FINISHED SIZE: ¹⁄₂" (1.5 cm)

TECHNIQUES USED
Balling (18), spiraling (22), hammering (17), oxidizing (27)

materials
Two 2¹⁄₂" (6.5 cm) pieces of sterling silver 20-gauge wire

tools
Torch
Round-nose pliers
Flat-nose pliers
Ball-peen hammer
Metal file
Liver of sulfur

resources
Wire: Metalliferous.

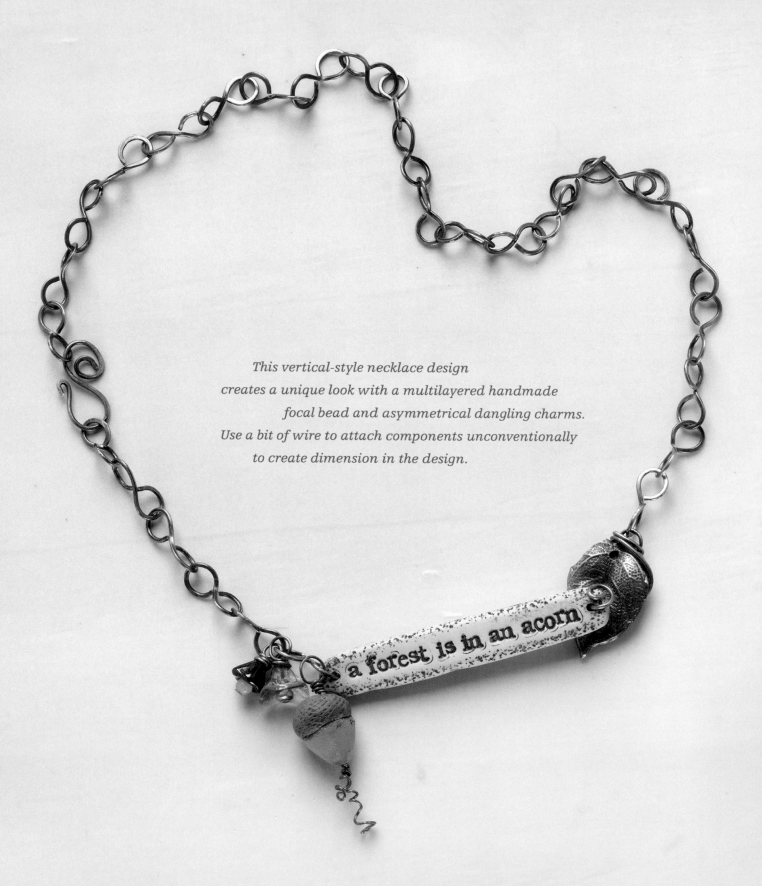

This vertical-style necklace design
creates a unique look with a multilayered handmade
focal bead and asymmetrical dangling charms.
Use a bit of wire to attach components unconventionally
to create dimension in the design.

a forest is in an acorn

A Forest Necklace

DESIGNED BY **Lorelei Eurto**

1. Cut twenty-nine 1¼" (3.2 cm) pieces of brass wire. Make 29 figure-eight links and hammer them flat.

2. Holding one loop of a figure-eight link with your fingers, grasp the other loop with the flat-nose pliers. Twist ¼ turn so that the loops sit perpendicular to each other. Repeat with the remaining 28 figure-eight links and join them together into a 23-piece chain and another 5-piece chain.

3. Cut 2¼" (5.5 cm) of brass wire. Form a small spiral hook. Attach the wire hook to the 23-piece chain and hook it to the 5-piece chain.

4. Curl the end of the copper wire several times around the tip of the round-nose pliers. String the acorn bead onto the copper wire and push it down to the curled wire.

5. Make a wrapped loop above the acorn, wrapping the wire 4 times. Bend the remaining copper wire down around the acorn bead. Wrap it around the curled wire below several times, then curl the remaining wire with the round-nose pliers.

6. Attach the left hole in the polymer quote pendant and the acorn charm to the end of the 5-piece chain.

7. String 1 brass spacer and 1 flower bead onto a head pin and make a wrapped loop. Repeat with the jade round and second flower bead. Attach these 2 charms to the chain link above the acorn charm.

8. Cut 2½" (6.5 cm) of brass wire. Form a spiral on one end using round-nose pliers. Thread the wire through the right hole in the polymer quote pendant and through the hole in the center of the pewter leaf charm. Pull the wire up and around the back of the leaf and wrap it around the top loop on the leaf charm. Tuck in the end of the wire with the flat-nose pliers.

9. Attach the end of the 23-piece chain to the loop on the leaf charm.

LEVEL 1

FINISHED SIZE: 21" (53.5 cm)

TECHNIQUES USED
Figure-eight links (19), hammering (17), spiral hooks (25), wrapped loops (20)

materials
41" (1 m) of oxidized brass 20-gauge wire
4" (10 cm) of copper 24-gauge wire
1 pewter 18x30mm leaf connector
1 polymer 10x70mm quote connector
1 polymer 10x15mm acorn bead
2 brass 2" (5 cm) head pins
1 3mm brass spacer
2 glass flower beads
1 new jade 2mm round

tools
Flush cutters
Round-nose pliers
Flat-nose pliers
Ball-peen hammer
Steel bench block

resources
Pewter leaf charm: Lynn Davis. *Polymer quote pendant:* Heather Wynn. *Polymer acorn bead:* Humblebeads. *Glass flower beads and jade round:* Fusion Beads. *Brass and copper wire:* Patina Queen. *Brass head pins:* Vintaj Brass Co. *Brass spacers:* Hands of the Hills.

Napping A Nimbus Necklace

DESIGNED BY **Kerry Bogert**

The combination of soft, supple felt
and hollow-formed lampworked glass
blends opposites. Though nothing alike,
together they are dreamy.
The swirls of silver wire caging the wool beads
evoke cool breezes as the clouds float by.

1. Cut 5 pieces of 16g sterling silver wire to 4" (10 cm) lengths. File the ends smooth.

2. With the round-nose pliers, form a small loop at one end of the wire. Use the natural resistance of the wire to leave space between the rounds to form an open spiral. Continue spiraling until you reach the center of the wire. Flip the piece and repeat this step at the opposite end, coiling in the same direction toward the first coil, until the coils meet. Repeat for the remaining 4 lengths of wire.

3. With your hands, open the spirals enough to put a felted wool bead inside, caging the wool bead. Repeat with the remaining 4 spirals and wool beads.

4. Use the 20g silver wire to link together the caged wool beads and the hollow lampworked glass beads with wrapped loops, alternating wool and glass beads. Each link uses about 4" (10 cm) of wire. If the wool beads don't have holes in them, use wire cutters to snip one end of the 20g wire to a sharp point and push it through the wool bead like a needle. Situate the holes so that the wire spirals show on each side of the bead.

5. For the back of the neck, coil the turquoise wire around 8" (20.5 cm) of a 10" (25.5 cm) length of 16g silver wire. (Working directly from the spool of colored copper wire spool will create much less waste, but if you prefer to work with a cut length of wire, you will need about 8' [2.4 m].) Trim the colored wire ends and file if sharp.

6. Add 1 lampworked glass rondelle to the 16g sterling silver wire. With chain-nose pliers, bend a 45° angle in the wire, locking the rondelle in place. Trim excess 16g wire to ¾" (2 cm). With round nose pliers, form a simple loop.

7. Add the second lampworked glass rondelle to the other end of the 16g sterling silver wire. Again use chain-nose pliers to form a 45° bend in the wire, locking the bead in place. Do not trim this wire. With round-nose pliers, form a simple hook in the wire.

8. With the bench block and nylon mallet, hammer the arch of the hook just formed. Bend a gentle arch to form the back neck piece to the shape of your neck and hammer that with the nylon or rawhide mallet.

9. Add a second layer of wrapped wire to the coiled wire strap. Wrap an 18" (45.5 cm) piece of 20g flag-blue-colored copper wire randomly over the turquoise wire, anchoring it on each end with 3 tight coils. Trim excess wire.

10. With chain-nose pliers, open the simple-loop side of the necklace strap and connect it to the first wrapped loop in the beaded strand. Close the simple loop.

11. With chain-nose pliers, open the colored wire jump ring, link it to the last wrapped loop in the beaded strand, and close the loop. This jump ring acts as the other half of the clasp.

LEVEL 2

FINISHED SIZE: 21½" (54.5 cm)

TECHNIQUES USED

Simple loops (19), spiraling (22), wrapped loops (20), coiling (22), hammering (17), simple hooks (24)

materials

30" (76 cm) of sterling silver 16-gauge half-hard wire

3' (91.5 cm) of sterling silver 20-gauge dead-soft wire

8' (2.4 m) or a spool of turquoise-colored copper 20-gauge wire

18" (45.5 cm) of flag-blue-colored copper 20-gauge wire

1 blue-colored wire 6mm jump ring

4 blue 15x20mm lampworked glass hollow beads

2 blue 5x8mm lampworked glass rondelles

3 blue 20mm felted wool beads

2 light blue 15mm felted wool beads

tools

Round-nose pliers

Chain-nose pliers

Flush cutters

Metal file

Steel bench block

Nylon or rawhide mallet

resources

Colored wire: Paramount Wire Co. *Lampworked and felt beads:* Kab's Creative Concepts. *Colored wire jump ring:* Blue Buddha Boutique.

Simple U-shaped wire elements help focus your attention on the beautiful handmade lampworked glass beads. Hammering the wire will ensure that the curved wire stays strong.

Suspended Drops Earrings

DESIGNED BY **Lorelei Eurto**

1. Cut two 2" (5 cm) pieces of wire. Cut two 1" (2.5 cm) pieces.
2. Curve 1 wire around the Sharpie marker to form a U shape. Trim the ends of the wire so that both ends are the same length. Form a simple parallel loop at both ends of the wire.
3. Hammer the curved section of wire flat.
4. Thread a 1" (2.5 cm) piece of wire through the left loop of the U-shaped piece. String 2 brass spacers, 1 lampworked drop, and 2 brass spacers. Thread the end of the wire through the right hole in the U-shaped piece.
5. Using the round-nose pliers, curve the ends of the straight wire down, creating a tight simple loop on each end. Attach the earring wire to the curved section of wire.
6. Repeat Steps 2–5 for the second earring.

LEVEL 1 ●

FINISHED SIZE: 2" (5 cm)

TECHNIQUES USED
Simple loops (19), hammering (17)

materials

8" (20.5 cm) of oxidized brass 20-gauge wire

2 blue lampworked glass 10x12mm drop beads

8 brass 3mm spacers

2 brass French ear wires

tools

Flush cutters

Round-nose pliers

Large Sharpie marker

Ball-peen hammer

Steel bench block

resources

Lampworked glass drops: Kelley's Beads. *Brass spacers:* Hands of the Hills. *Earring wires:* Vintaj Brass Co. *Brass wire:* Patina Queen.

*Heavy-gauge wire hammered flat
makes a bold statement.
Flattening and texturing 14-gauge wire
makes it look more like sheet metal,
and piercing the ends for
the jump ring is a simple cold connection.*

Popular Mechanics Earrings

DESIGNED BY **Denise Peck**

1. Using the flat side of the ball-peen hammer, flatten the entire length of 14g wire.

2. Using a texturing hammer or the thin end of a riveting hammer, texture the length of flattened wire.

3. Use the torch to anneal the wire.

4. Cut the wire in half and use the awl and hammer (or hole punch) to punch a hole $1/16$" (2mm) from one end on both pieces.

5. Fold both pieces in half over the ballpoint pen so the ends meet. Push the awl through the first hole to mark the other end where the second hole will go. Punch the second hole in each piece.

6. Open the links and add the glass donuts. Close the links and add 2 linked jump rings to each.

7. Add ear wires to the jump rings.

LEVEL 2 ● ●

FINISHED SIZE: 2" (5 cm)

TECHNIQUES USED
Hammering (17), annealing (18), piercing (17)

materials

5" (12.5 cm) of fine silver 14-gauge wire
4 silver 6mm 20-gauge jump rings
2 lampworked glass 20mm large-hole donuts
2 silver French ear wires

tools

Round-nose pliers
Chain-nose pliers
Flush cutters
Awl or metal hole punch
Ball-peen hammer
Steel bench block
Texturing or riveting hammer
Ballpoint pen
Butane torch

resources

Lampworked glass donuts: Beads of Passion.

*Forming wire links to attach different
components together in this bracelet design
adds to its originality.
The spring blue and yellow color palette
is versatile for any season.*

Bubbling Bracelet

DESIGNED BY **Lorelei Eurto**

1. Cut 3" (7.5 cm) of 20g wire. Form a wrapped loop at one end. String 1 lampworked glass hollow bead. Form a wrapped loop with the remaining wire.

2. Attach 1 large chain link to each wrapped loop. Attach 1 pewter ring connector to each chain link.

3. Silver wire links: Cut two 2" (5 cm) pieces of silver wire. Center 1 piece on the widest part of the round-nose pliers and bend it in a U shape. Make a simple loop on each end. Repeat with the second wire. Thread one U-shaped wire through each pewter ring connector and pinch the ends of each wire in toward each other. Attach 4 jump rings around the 2 pinched wire ends of each U-shaped piece.

4. Attach 1 etched cable chain link to each simple loop on one of the silver wire links. Attach the end length of a 4-link section of etched chain through both links.

5. Use a jump ring to connect the ceramic circle charm to the other end of the chain.

6. Fold the 4" (10 cm) section of link chain in half. Attach each end of the chain to one of the simple loops on the other silver wire connector.

7. Use the 2" (5 cm) section of steel wire to create a spiral hook with a small, slightly squared spiral portion and attach it the end of the chain links.

8. String 1 ceramic cube bead and 1 copper seed bead onto a head pin. Form a wrapped loop. Repeat to make a second cube bead charm.

9. String 1 copper seed bead, 1 blue glass spacer, and 1 yellow glass spacer onto a head pin. Form a wrapped loop. Repeat to make a second glass spacer charm.

10. Attach 1 glass spacer charm and 1 cube bead charm to the large chain link on each side of the hollow bead.

LEVEL 1

FINISHED SIZE: 8 1/2" (21.5 cm)

TECHNIQUES USED
Wrapped loops (20), simple loops (19), spiral hooks (25), opening and closing jump rings (23)

materials

9" (23 cm) of sterling silver 20-gauge dead-soft round wire

1 1/2" (3.8 cm) of galvanized steel 19-gauge wire

4 silver 2" (5 cm) head pins

2 silver 15mm chain links

9 silver-plated brass 7mm jump rings

4" (10 cm) of silver-plated brass link chain

1 3/4" (2 cm) of silver-plated etched cable chain

1 blue 15x20mm lampworked glass hollow bead

2 pewter 12mm ring connectors

1 ceramic 10mm circle charm

2 ceramic 10mm cube beads

2 yellow 5mm lampworked glass spacers

2 blue 5mm lampworked glass spacers

4 oxidized copper size 6° metal seed beads

tools

Round-nose pliers

Flat-nose pliers

Flush cutters

resources

Lampworked glass hollow: Kab's Creative Concepts. *Lampworked glass spacers:* Studio Rent. *Ceramic charm and cubes:* Elaine Ray. *Pewter ring connectors:* Green Girl Studios. *Jump rings and chain:* AD Adornments. *Copper metal seed beads:* Bello Modo.

Siren's Song Necklace

DESIGNED BY **Cindy Wimmer**

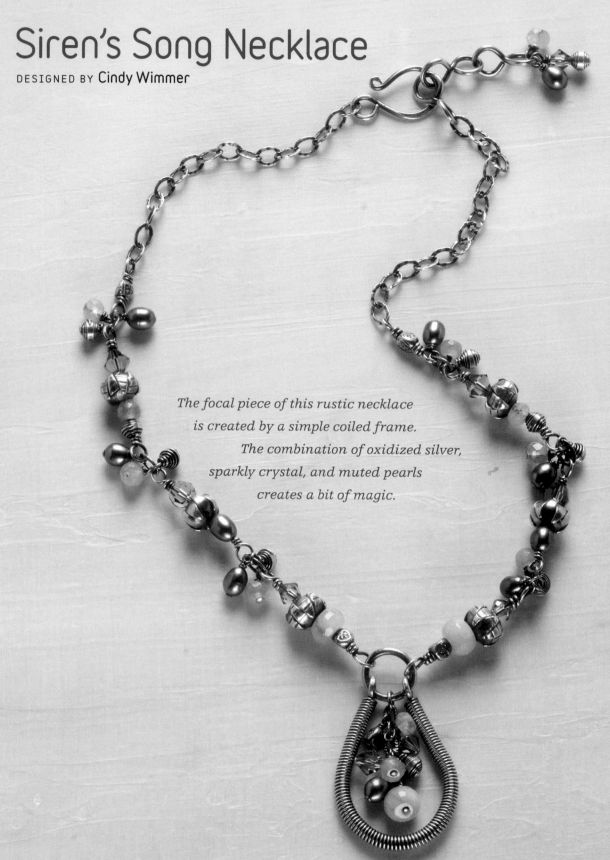

*The focal piece of this rustic necklace
is created by a simple coiled frame.
The combination of oxidized silver,
sparkly crystal, and muted pearls
creates a bit of magic.*

1. Wrap the 14g wire around an 8mm mandrel to create a 10mm OD jump ring. Set aside. Cut 6 individual links from the 5×6mm hammered chain. Set aside.

2. Coil the 22g wire around the 2mm mandrel for 2⅞" (7.5 cm). Cut a 4½" (1.5 cm) length of 16g wire. Slide the coil onto the 16g wire. Form a simple loop on each end of the wire with small round-nose pliers and center the loops.

3. Place a 20mm mandrel on the center of the coil and bend up the ends, forming a horseshoe shape. Open the simple loops and attach both to the 10mm jump ring.

4. Cut a 5-link section from the 3×4mm chain. String 1 aquamarine 8mm rondelle on a head pin and attach it to the end of the chain with a wrapped loop. Attach 2 aquamarine 6mm rondelles, 1 pearl, 1 Swarovski 6mm bicone, 1 Swarovski 4mm bicone, 1 three-sided bead, and 1 rolled spacer along the sides of the chain with head pins. Attach the end of the chain to the 10mm jump ring with the 4mm jump ring.

5. Using a 3¼" (8.3 cm) piece of 20g wire, form a wrapped loop around the 10mm jump ring. String 1 triangular spacer, 1 aquamarine 8mm rondelle, 1 round leaf bead, and 1 Swarovski 4mm bicone. Form a wrapped loop to join a single link of hammered chain. With another 3¼" (8.3 cm) piece of 20g wire, form a second wrapped loop around the same hammered link. String 1 pearl, 1 round leaf bead, and 1 Swarovski 6mm round. Attach it to a second hammered link with a wrapped loop. With a 3¼" (8.3 cm) piece of 20g wire, form a second wrapped loop around the second link of hammered chain. String 1 rolled spacer bead, 1 aquamarine 6mm rondelle, 1 round leaf bead, and 1 Swarovski 6mm bicone. Attach to a third hammered link with a wrapped loop. With a 2" (5 cm) piece of 20g wire, form a wrapped loop around the third hammered link, string 1 triangular bead, and attach a 3" (7.5 cm) length of 5×6mm chain with a wrapped loop. Repeat entire step for the opposite side of the necklace.

6. Using a separate head pin for each, attach 1 rice pearl, 1 rolled spacer, and 1 aquamarine 6mm rondelle to each of the single hammered links with wrapped loops to create dangles.

7. Cut three 2" (5 cm) lengths of 16g wire. Create 3 figure-eight links. Attach them to create an extender chain. Attach this extender chain to one end of the hammered chain. With 2½" (6.5 cm) of 16g wire, create a simple hook and attach it to the other end of the hammered chain. Using a separate head pin for each, attach 1 aquamarine 6mm rondelle, 1 pearl, 1 Swarovski bicone, and 1 rolled spacer to the end of the extender chain with wrapped loops.

8. Dip the necklace in liver of sulfur solution and then buff with steel wool. Clean with a polishing cloth.

LEVEL 2

FINISHED SIZE: 17" (43 cm)

TECHNIQUES USED

Making jump rings (23), coiling (22), simple loops (19), wrapped loops (20), figure-eight links (19), simple hooks (24), oxidizing (27)

materials

2' (61 cm) of sterling silver 20-gauge half-hard wire

3' (.9 m) of sterling silver 22-gauge half-hard wire

13" (33 cm) of sterling silver 16-gauge dead-soft wire

2" (5 cm) of sterling silver 14-gauge dead-soft wire

10 blue-gray 5–6mm rice pearls

2 blue sapphire 6mm Swarovski crystal rounds

4 blue sapphire 4mm Swarovski crystal bicones

3 blue sapphire 6mm Swarovski crystal bicones

11 aquamarine 6mm faceted rondelles

3 aquamarine 8mm faceted rondelles

10 hill tribe silver 4mm rolled spacers

5 hill tribe silver 4–5mm three-sided beads

6 hill tribe silver 7x9mm round leaf bead

9" of hammered link 5x6mm chain

⅝" of 3x4mm chain

1 sterling silver 4mm jump ring

1 sterling silver 10mm jump ring

29 sterling silver 24-gauge head pins

tools

Small round-nose pliers

Chain-nose pliers

Flush cutters

8mm mandrel

20mm mandrel (punches from a disc cutter set or a wooden dowel work well)

Bead reamer (optional; for pearls)

Ball-peen hammer

Steel bench block

2mm steel mandrel

Liver of sulfur (optional)

Fine steel wool, #0000 (optional)

Polishing cloth

resources

Rice pearls: Jewelry Supply. *Hill tribe beads*: A Silver Planet.

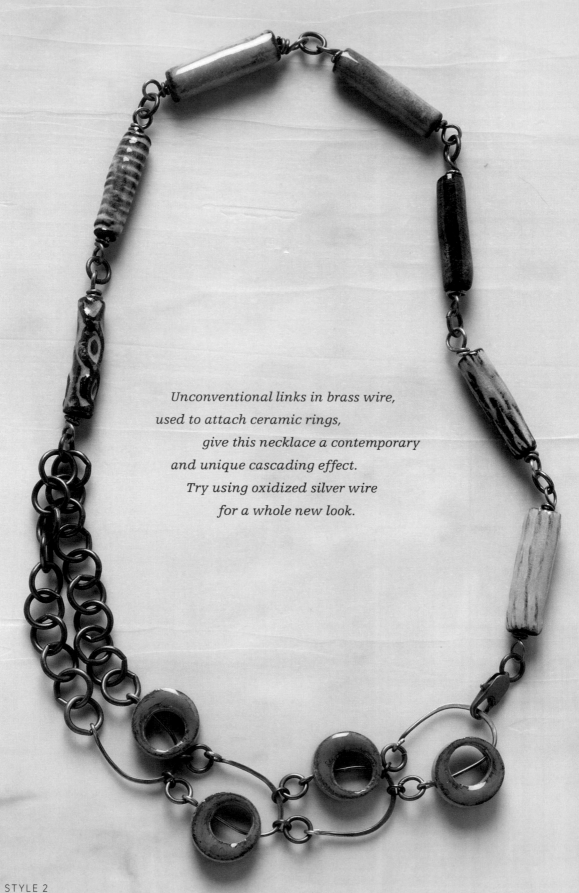

Unconventional links in brass wire,
used to attach ceramic rings,
give this necklace a contemporary
and unique cascading effect.
Try using oxidized silver wire
for a whole new look.

Cascading Rings Necklace

DESIGNED BY **Lorelei Eurto**

① Cut four 2" (5 cm) pieces of 20g wire. Curve each wire around the Sharpie marker, forming a U shape. String 1 ceramic ring bead onto one side of the U shape. Lightly hammer the curve and the side of the U shape without the bead. Form a simple loop on each end of the wire parallel to each other. Repeat for the remaining 3 ceramic ring beads.

② Attach a 4mm jump ring to each simple loop on the bottom of the U-shaped links. Attach a 7mm jump ring to each 4mm jump ring and connect to a simple loop of another U-shaped link. Alternate the ring beads so that the beads sit on alternate sides.

③ Fold the 6" (15 cm) section of chain in half and attach each end link to one of the simple loops on the end of the cascading rings section.

④ Attach a 7mm jump ring to the end of the chain section.

⑤ Cut seven 2½" (6.5 cm) pieces of 20g wire. With 1 piece, form a wrapped loop. String 1 tube bead. Form another wrapped loop on the other end of the bead. Repeat for the remaining 6 tube beads. Join the links using 7mm jump rings.

⑥ Attach a 7mm jump ring to the end of the tube bead section and attach the brass lobster clasp. To fasten the necklace, attach the lobster clasp to the last U connector at the curved side.

LEVEL 1 ●

FINISHED SIZE: 21½" (54.5 cm)

TECHNIQUES USED
Hammering (17), simple loops (19), opening and closing jump rings (23), wrapped loops (20)

materials
26" (66 cm) of oxidized brass 20-gauge wire
7 ceramic 30mm tube beads
4 blue ceramic 18mm ring beads
14 brass 7mm jump rings
6" (12.5 cm) of brass 10mm round-link chain
1 brass 12mm lobster clasp
6 brass 4mm jump rings

tools
Round-nose pliers
Chain-nose pliers
Flat-nose pliers
Flush cutters
Ball-peen hammer
Steel bench block
Large Sharpie marker

resources
Ceramic beads: Elaine Ray. *Brass chain and findings:* Vintaj Brass Co. *Brass wire:* Patina Queen.

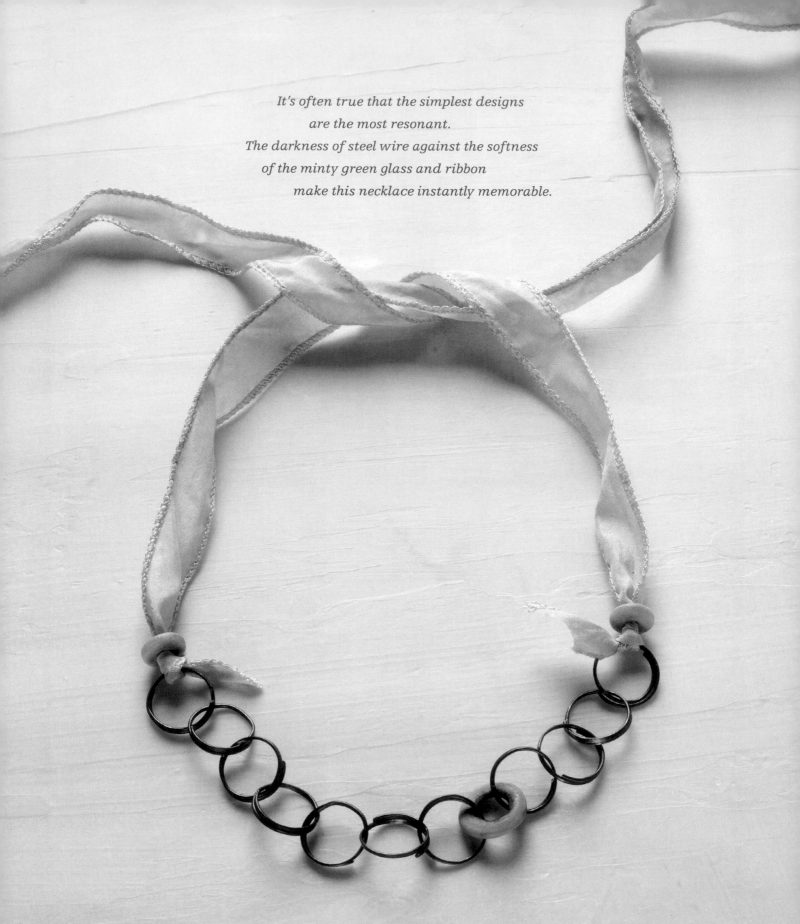

It's often true that the simplest designs
are the most resonant.
The darkness of steel wire against the softness
of the minty green glass and ribbon
make this necklace instantly memorable.

Breaking Rhythm Necklace

DESIGNED BY **Denise Peck**

1. Wind the steel wire around the mandrel to make a tight coil of 18 wraps.

2. Cut apart the coils into split rings, each ring 1½ full loops, for a total of 10 rings.

3. Join 4 of the rings together into a chain. Add the porcelain donut to the fourth ring. Add the fifth ring to the porcelain donut. Add the 5 remaining rings onto the chain.

4. Cut the ribbon in half. Tie the cut sides to either end of the chain.

5. Slide a small porcelain disc bead onto each side of the ribbon, pushing them down to sit atop the knots. Close the necklace by tying the ribbons together behind the neck.

LEVEL 2

FINISHED SIZE: 24" (61 cm)

TECHNIQUES USED
Coiling (22)

materials

1 spool annealed steel 19-gauge round wire
1 porcelain 15mm donut
2 porcelain 10mm disc beads
42" (107 cm) silk ribbon

tools

Round-nose pliers
Chain-nose pliers
Heavy-duty flush cutters
1/2" mandrel or wood dowel

resources

Steel wire: Sears. *Porcelain beads:* Joan Miller Porcelain Beads.

The big swirl hook becomes a focal piece
in this all–sterling-silver bangle.
Create the base of the bracelet
and the hook clasp
with just one length of wire!

Change of Heart Bangle

DESIGNED BY **Cindy Wimmer**

1. Cut a 5½' (1.7 m) length of 20g wire and coil it on the steel mandrel until it reaches 5¾" (14.5 cm) in length. Trim the wire and set the coil aside.

2. Flush cut both ends of the 14g wire. For the clasp, begin by hammering ¼" (6 mm) on one end of the wire. With the tip of the small round-nose pliers, make a very small simple loop. Make a small hook and then hammer the curve.

3. Hold a 14mm mandrel alongside the hook. Press the wire up and around the mandrel, forming a complete circle. Insert the 12mm mandrel into the circle, wrapping the wire around it to create a second circle inside of the first. Stop forming the second circle before you reach the top of the first circle. Hammer the entire clasp slightly.

4. Using the flat-nose pliers, bend the wire 90° so the wire is now perpendicular to the clasp. Using your wrist or a bracelet mandrel, shape the wire into a bangle. Slide on the 5¾" (14.5 cm) coil and then the hammered heart bead.

5. Measure ⅞" (2.2 cm) from the heart bead and trim. Using the back of the large round-nose pliers, make a simple loop. Center the loop and hammer.

6. Starting behind the clasp, wrap the remaining 20g wire several times to the bracelet to secure. Continue wrapping the wire around the frame, randomly adding 3mm round beads. When the end is reached, wrap the wire around the frame several times to secure, then trim. Repeat with the 22g wire, starting at the base of the heart bead. Wrap the 22g wire close to the 20g wire, wrapping several times to secure once the end is reached.

7. Dip the bracelet in liver of sulfur solution and then buff with steel wool. Place in a rotary tumbler to work-harden and polish.

LEVEL 2

FINISHED SIZE: 7½" (19 cm)

TECHNIQUES USED
Coiling (22), hammering (17), simple loops (19), simple hooks (24), oxidizing (27)

materials

12" (30.5 cm) of sterling silver 14-gauge dead-soft wire

7½' (2.3 mm) of sterling silver 20-gauge half-hard wire

2' (61 cm) of sterling silver 22-gauge half-hard wire

30–40 sterling silver 3mm round beads

16x18mm hill tribe silver hammered heart

tools

Large round-nose pliers
Small round-nose pliers
Flat-nose pliers
Flush cutters
Ball-peen hammer
Steel bench block
2mm steel mandrel
12mm and 14mm mandrel (or wooden dowels)
Liver of sulfur (optional)
Fine steel wool, #0000 (optional)
Polishing cloth
Rotary tumbler

resources

3mm round sterling silver beads: Artbeads.
Hill tribe hammered heart bead: SII Findings.

These unique cupped lampworked glass beads
give this necklace a wonderful fullness
without bulk and make the sweetest
little tinkling sound as you walk.

Departing Arrival Necklace

DESIGNED BY **Kerry Bogert**

1 Using 3" (7.5 cm) of 18g wire and chain-nose pliers, form a 90° bend in the wire about 2" (5 cm) from one end. Grasp the longer side of the wire with the tip of the round-nose pliers next to the bend. With your dominant hand, begin a spiral around the tip of the pliers, then continue to spiral from the center out, making 2½–3 complete turns. Use wire cutters to trim the spiral. Repeat to make a total of 18 wire head pins.

2 String a lampworked glass disc bead onto the wire head pin and with round-nose pliers, form a simple loop with the wire on the backside of the disc. Repeat for 17 more disc beads.

3 Repeat Step 2 with the glass head pins and the remaining lampworked glass discs.

4 With chain-nose pliers, open the simple loop on the back of a disc bead and attach it to one of the center links in the cable chain. Close the loop. Repeat to add the rest of the beads to the chain, placing the larger beads in the center and adding the smaller ones as you work out to each side. (The beads will attach to about 8" [20.5 cm] of the chain.)

5 Make a simple hook from the 16-gauge wire and attach to one end of the chain. Make a figure-eight link and attach it to the other end of the chain.

LEVEL 2

FINISHED SIZE: 17½" (44.5 cm)

TECHNIQUES USED
Spiraling (22), simple loops (19), simple hooks (24), figure-eight links (19)

materials
4½' (1.4 m) of sterling silver 18-gauge dead-soft wire
6" (15 cm) of sterling silver 16-gauge dead-soft wire
18 glass head pins
36 lampworked glass discs in graduated sizes
18" (45.5 cm) of gunmetal-colored cable chain

tools
Chain-nose pliers
Round-nose pliers
Flush cutters

resources
Lampworked glass beads and glass head pins: Kab's Creative Concepts. Gunmetal-colored chain: Etsy.

Hammered and polished silver wire wraps its way around your finger with style. This simple ring is easy to create and makes a very bold, modern statement.

Budding Ring

DESIGNED BY **Donna Spadafore**

① Cut the 18g wire into 2 pieces, one 3½" (9 cm) and the other 3¾" (9.5 cm). Ball up both ends of all 3 pieces of wire using the torch.

② Hammer the balls on both ends of both 18g wires flat. If the flattened ends on the 18g wires are not facing the same direction, hold each end in a pair of pliers and twist slightly until they face the same direction. Hammer the full length of the two 18g wires flat.

③ With pliers, bend the wires just behind the flattened balls so that they sit at a slight angle to the middle portion of the wire. Make sure to make the bends so that both point in the same direction.

④ Hammer the balled ends of the 22g wire flat. Cut the wire in half.

⑤ Hold the 18g wires together so that the bends in the ends face opposite directions from each other. The wires should be held so that the ends are slightly offset from each other.

⑥ Bind the 18g wires together with the 22g wires as follows: Hold the flattened end of one 22g wire next to the flattened ends of the 18g wire on the front side of the ring and wrap it around 4 times to show on the front. Trim the 22g wire on the back. Repeat at the other end of the 18g wires.

⑦ Wrap the joined wires around a ring mandrel, making sure that the flattened ends of the 22g wire are facing outward. Start shaping the ring at a very small diameter and push the ring down the mandrel to stretch it to the correct size.

LEVEL 2 ●●

FINISHED SIZE: 2¼" (5.5 cm)

TECHNIQUES USED
Hammering (17), balling (18)

materials
7¼" (18.5 cm) of silver 18-gauge round wire
5" (12.5 cm) silver 22-gauge round wire

tools
Torch
Flat-nose pliers
Ball-peen hammer
Bench block
Ring mandrel

resources
Wire: Metalliferous.

Black chain and annealed steel wire
pair beautifully in these whimsical earrings.
Add a favorite bead to dangle
from the tangle of wire for a jolt of color.

Tumbleweed Earrings

DESIGNED BY **Denise Peck**

1 Working from the spool, coil the steel wire 2 times around the closed jaws of the round-nose pliers. Slip the double loop off the pliers and begin wrapping around the middle, perpendicular to the original loops. Wrap sloppily until there is a tangle of wire around the two inside loops.

2 Cut a length of 10 links of black chain. Open the last link as though opening a jump ring and attach it to the two center loops of one end of the tumbleweed link.

3 Attach the ear wire to the other end of the 5-link chain.

4 Repeat Steps 1–3 for the second earring.

LEVEL 1 ●
FINISHED SIZE: 2" (5 cm)
TECHNIQUES USED
Coiling (22), opening and closing jump rings (23)

materials
1 spool of annealed steel 26-gauge wire
20 links of black 1x2mm chain
2 gunmetal ear wires

tools
Chain-nose pliers
Round-nose pliers
Heavy-duty flush cutters

resources
Annealed steel wire: Sears. *Ear wire:* Artbeads.
Chain: AD Adornments.

Over the moon about metal, that is.
    Wire, sheet metal, scrap metal,
rusty metal, you name it.
    For metal enthusiasts,
this project will give you practice
    in the fine art of flattening wire.

Over the Moon Bracelet

DESIGNED BY **Connie Fox**

1. Make the base chain by connecting each 10mm jump ring to the next with two 5mm jump rings.

2. Cut 2" (5 cm) of the 14g silver wire and set aside. With a ball-peen hammer, hit the brass and 14g silver wire dead-on to flatten and keep it straight. (If you hammer more to one side of the wire, it will curve away from the hammering. To correct this, hammer in the concave area until the wire straightens out.) Hammer until the wire is thin enough to bend with pliers but still retains the strength of the metal.

3. Cut three 1" (2.5 cm) pieces of the brass wire and set aside. Using the round-nose and chain-nose pliers, make 6 free-form dangles with the remaining flattened brass wire. Finish each with a simple loop.

4. Hammer each end of the three 1" (2.5 cm) pieces of brass wire flatter so that the ends spread out into a dog-bone shape. Pierce one end of each with an awl. Coil 24-gauge silver wire around the middle of each dog-bone charm.

5. Make 4 free-form dangles from the flattened silver wire that are slightly larger than the brass dangles. Finish each with a simple loop.

6. Cut the 18g silver wire into five 1" (2.5 cm) pieces. Make a simple loop on the end of one piece, string a hill tribe bead onto the piece, and finish with a simple loop. Repeat for each of the other four 1" pieces.

7. Clean the brass stampings with a fine sanding sponge or abrasive paper. Texture each stamping with a hammer, design punches, or center punch. Pierce each one near an edge to accommodate a jump ring and file the burr from the back.

8. File any burrs or sharp edges from the components. Connect each charm to the bracelet with a 5mm jump ring. Use the 2" (5 cm) piece of silver wire from Step 2 to make a simple hook. Attach it to one end of the bracelet with a 5mm jump ring.

9. Dip the bracelet in liver of sulfur solution and then buff with steel wool.

LEVEL 2

FINISHED SIZE: 7½" (19 cm)

TECHNIQUES USED
Hammering (17), simple loops (19), piercing (17), coiling (22), oxidizing (27), simple hooks (24)

materials

20" (51 cm) of sterling silver 14 gauge dead-soft wire

18" (45.5 cm) of brass 14-gauge wire

5" of sterling silver 18-gauge half-hard wire

6' of 24-gauge sterling silver dead-soft wire

5 brass 24-gauge stampings

5 hill tribe silver 6x8mm beads

12 sterling silver 14-gauge 10mm ID jump rings

45 sterling silver 16-gauge 5mm ID jump rings

tools

Flat-nose pliers

Chain-nose pliers

Small round-nose pliers

Long round-nose pliers

Flush cutters

Flat needle file

Ball-peen hammer

Anvil or large steel bench block

Nylon or rawhide mallet

Awl

Center punch

Fine sanding sponge or abrasive paper

Texture tools (hammer, center punch, design stamps)

Liver of sulfur (optional)

Fine steel wool, #0000 (optional)

resources

All materials: Jatayu.

Create a classic design
with heavy-gauge copper wire.
With its repeating pattern
and twisted wire texture,
this necklace has a timeless appeal.

Octavia Necklace

DESIGNED BY **Cindy Wimmer**

① Wind 11" (28 cm) of 16g wire into coils on the 5mm mandrel. Cut the coils into 11 jump rings. Wind 12" (30.5 cm) of 20g twisted copper wire into coils on the 5mm mandrel. Cut the coils into 11 jump rings.

② Wind the 22g twisted wire on a 2mm mandrel. Cut one 1½" (3.8 cm) length for the hook clasp and set aside. Cut the remaining twisted wire coils into eleven ⅞" (2.2 cm) lengths.

③ Flush cut 11 pieces of 16g wire to 7½" (19 cm) lengths. Hammer the end of the wire slightly and make a loop with the end of the small round-nose pliers. Hold the loop with the flat-nose pliers and begin to coil the wire into a loose spiral (so that the wires do not touch as they spiral around). Make 3 rotations.

④ Grasp the tail wire in the back of the small round-nose pliers. Bend the wire up and around the pliers, removing the pliers and reinserting them to create a complete loop.

⑤ Hammer the spiral with the ball-peen hammer to flatten. Hammer with the rounded side to add texture. Reshape the spiral if needed.

⑥ Slide on a ⅞" (2.2 cm) twisted wire coil and shape the tail around the outside of the hammered spiral by pressing around the outside curve. Measure the end of the bare wire tail and trim to ¾" (2 cm). Using the back of the round-nose pliers, roll the wire to form a simple loop.

⑦ Repeat Steps 3–6 for each of the 11 pieces, making sure that the orientation of the spiral links is the same for each.

⑧ Cut 2⅝" (6.5 cm) of 16g wire. Create a simple loop with the back of the round-nose pliers. Slide on the reserved 1½" (3.8 cm) twisted wire coil. Make a small loop at the other end with the tip of round-nose pliers and bend around a dowel or pen to create a hook. Create a figure-eight link with 16g wire for the eye of the clasp.

⑨ Link the spirals together with 2 jump rings, one simple and one twisted. Attach the hook to one end and the figure-eight link to the other end.

⑩ Dip the necklace in liver of sulfur solution and then buff with steel wool. Place in a rotary tumbler to work-harden and polish.

LEVEL 2

FINISHED SIZE: 17" (43 cm)

TECHNIQUES USED
Coiling (22), making jump rings (23), flush cutting (17), hammering (17), simple loops (19), spiraling (22), simple hooks (24), figure-eight links (19), oxidizing (27)

materials
12" (30.5 cm) of copper 20-gauge twisted wire
12' (3.7 m) of copper 22-gauge twisted wire
9' (2.7 m) of 16-gauge copper wire

tools
Large round-nose pliers
Small round-nose pliers
Flat-nose pliers
Flush cutters
Ball-peen hammer
Steel bench block
2mm and 5mm mandrels
Liver of sulfur (optional)
Fine steel wool, #0000 (optional)
Polishing cloth
Rotary tumbler

resources
Twisted copper wire: Fundametals.

This pendant is made from
two frames linked together
with fine wire.
Adding semiprecious stone beads
adds an easy elegance
to the simple design.

Semiprecious Paisley Necklace

DESIGNED BY Jodi Bombardier

1. Straighten and flush cut two 3" (7.5 cm) pieces of 16g wire for the frame.

2. With round-nose pliers, make a small loop at the end of the wire, then continue to loop around another ¼ turn to begin a loose spiral. To avoid twisting the square wire, make a quarter of the loop, then remove the pliers and reinsert them into the loop from the opposite side to finish making the loop. Make another loop and spiral on the other end of the wire with the loop going in the opposite direction. Repeat entire step with the second 3" (7.5 cm) piece of 16g wire.

3. Cut 3' (.9 m) of 26g wire. Coil one of the frame wires from halfway inside the top loop to halfway inside the bottom loop. Cut the wire tails.

4. Place the frame wires on a flat surface, positioned with two loops back-to-back so that one side of the frame is higher than the other and the bottom two loops sit atop each other. Tape the bottom of the frame wires together.

5. Cut 3' (.9 m) of 26g wire. Leaving a 2' (61 cm) tail, wrap the top of the 2 frames together 2 times, then continue to coil up the bare frame wire to halfway inside the loop. Trim the end of the wire within the loop.

6. Slide a bead or pearl onto the 2' (61 cm) tail of 26g wire and wrap the 2 frame wires together 2–4 times. Continue adding beads to the wire randomly and coiling the down the single bare frame wire, positioning the beads to sit on the front of the piece.

7. Remove the tape as needed. At the bottom of the frames, wrap the 2 frames together where each loop touches the opposite frame wire. Cut the wire tail.

8. Cut two 9" (23 cm) lengths of sterling silver chain. Attach each piece of chain with a separate jump ring to the space at the top of the frame between the coiled loop and where the first bead is attached. With jump rings, attach the toggle clasp to the other ends of the chains.

LEVEL 3 ● ● ●

FINISHED SIZE: 21" (53 cm)

TECHNIQUES USED
Straightening wire (17), flush cutting (17), simple loops (19), coiling (22), opening and closing jump rings (23)

materials
9" (23 cm) of sterling silver 16-gauge dead-soft square wire
6' (1.8 m) of sterling silver 26-gauge dead-soft round wire
8–10 peridot 4mm faceted rondelle beads
8–10 sapphire 4mm faceted rondelle beads
10–12 freshwater pearls, 3mm
18" (45.5 cm) of sterling silver oval chain
4 sterling silver 6mm 18-gauge jump rings
1 toggle clasp

tools
Flush cutters
Chain-nose pliers
Round-nose pliers
Wire-straightening pliers
Ruler
Sharpie fine-tip marker
Low-stick tape

resources
Semiprecious stones: TAJ Company. *Sterling silver wire:* Indian Jewelers Supply. *Sterling silver chain:* SII Findings. *Freshwater pearls:* local bead store. *Jump rings:* Rio Grande. *Clasp:* Tierra Cast.

A few simple twists make the perfect frame for showcasing a bead. These stay simple with a coordinating silver spacer, but add any favorite bead to personalize the design.

Silver Lassos Earrings

DESIGNED BY **Jane Dickerson**

1. Cut the twisted wire into two 6" (15 cm) pieces.
2. String 1 spacer bead on the wire. Using your fingers, gently cross one end of the wire over the straight portion, creating a teardrop loop around the spacer bead. With chain-nose pliers, wrap the short end of the wire around the straight portion 2 times. Trim the excess wire and tuck in the cut end with chain-nose pliers.
3. Create a second wrapped loop with the other end of the wire, leaving enough room to wrap the wire 3 times just above the previous wraps, for a total of 5 wraps. Trim the wire and tuck in the end.
4. Using chain-nose pliers, attach the dangle to the ear wire.
5. Repeat Steps 1–4 for the other earring.
6. Dip the necklace in liver of sulfur solution and then buff with steel wool.

LEVEL 1 ●

FINISHED SIZE: 1¹/₂" (3.8 cm)

TECHNIQUES USED
Wrapped loops (20), oxidizing (27)

materials

12" (30.5 cm) of sterling silver 24-gauge twisted wire

2 nickel-silver 6x3.5mm textured spacer beads

2 sterling silver ball-end ear wires

tools

Chain-nose pliers

Flush cutters

Liver of sulfur

Polishing cloth

Fine steel wool, #0000

resources

Twisted wire: Thunderbird Supply. *Spacer bead:* Silk Road Treasures. *Ear wires:* You and Me Findings. *Liver of sulfur and polishing cloth:* Rio Grande.

A head pin becomes a design element when you ball up the other end, too. Make a series of these links, attaching each to the next before wrapping for an unusual chain.

Still Waters Earrings
DESIGNED BY **Denise Peck**

1. Cut the 20g wire in half. Ball both ends on both pieces using the butane torch.

2. Make a mark with the marker ¾" (2 cm) from both ends of 1 piece of wire. Make a wrapped loop at each of the marks, sloppily wrapping the ends down the length of the link. Repeat on the second piece of wire.

3. Cut the 28g wire in half. Use each half to make a briolette loop on each disc bead.

4. Add jump rings to both ends of both links. Attach a briolette loop on one end of each link.

5. Add ear wires to the jump rings at the other ends of the links.

LEVEL 2 ● ●
FINISHED SIZE: 2" (5 cm)
TECHNIQUES USED
Balling (18), wrapped loops (20), opening and closing jump rings (23)

materials
5" (12.5 cm) of fine silver 20-gauge wire
4 silver 5mm 18- or 20-gauge jump rings
5" (12.5 cm) of sterling silver 28-gauge wire
2 lampworked glass 12mm disc beads
2 French ear wires

tools
Butane torch
Sharpie marker
Round-nose pliers
Chain-nose pliers
Flush cutters

resources
Lampworked glass disc beads: Boobie Beads.

*Looking for a new wire link
to add to your repertoire?
You'll have a new design favorite
when you see how these links
complement just about any bead set.*

Dash of Whimsy Bracelet

DESIGNED BY **Cindy Wimmer**

1 Coil the 22g wire tightly around the 2mm mandrel. Cut the coil into four 1¼" (3.2 cm) lengths. Cut the 18g wire into four 6" (15 cm) pieces. Cut the 16g wire into four 3" (7.5 cm) pieces. Set these aside.

2 Cut the 14g wire into four 2¼" (5.5 cm) pieces. With the Sharpie, mark the wires ¼" (6 mm) from each end. Grasp the wire on the mark with the back of the large round-nose pliers and roll forward, creating a loop as if to make an S-hook. Repeat on the other end of the wire in the opposite direction.

3 Hammer the outside curves of the link on a bench block to flatten. Reshape the link if necessary.

4 Slide a coil to the middle of a piece of 18g wire. Bend the wire in half, creating a U shape.

5 Place a link from Step 2 on top of the center of the U-shaped coil. Wrap each side of the coil tightly around the center of the link. Wrap the 18g wire tails around each side of the link and trim on the back side of the link. Repeat to create 4 bow-shaped links.

6 Slide a bead onto a piece of 16g wire. Add 2 spacers to each end and create simple loops with the small round-nose pliers. Repeat with the remaining 2 beads. Open the loops of the bead links and attach to the bow links, alternating bead and bow links to form a chain.

7 Create a simple hook with the remaining 14g wire. Hammer the curve of the hook, then attach it to the bow link at one end.

8 Dip the bracelet in liver of sulfur solution and then buff with steel wool. Place in a rotary tumbler to work-harden and polish.

LEVEL 3

FINISHED SIZE: 8¼" (21 cm)

TECHNIQUES USED
Coiling (22), hammering (17), simple loops (19), simple hooks (24), oxidizing (27)

materials

5' (1.5 m) of sterling silver 22-gauge half-hard wire

2' (61 cm) of sterling silver 18-gauge dead-soft wire

12" (30.5 m) of sterling silver 16-gauge dead-soft wire

12" (30.5 m) of sterling silver 14-gauge dead-soft wire

3 lampworked glass 18x18mm nugget beads

12 sterling silver 5mm spacers

tools

Large round-nose pliers

Small round-nose pliers

Chain-nose pliers

Flat-nose pliers

Flush cutters

2mm steel mandrel

Ball-peen hammer

Steel bench block

Black Sharpie marker

Liver of sulfur

Fine steel wool, #0000 (optional)

Polishing cloth

Rotary tumbler

resources

Lampworked glass nuggets: Moon Stumpp.

*Coils and spirals come together
in an everyday design.
This chain would make a wonderful base
for a fabulous charm bracelet.*

Full Circle Bracelet

DESIGNED BY **Lisa Niven Kelly**

1. Cut the 24g wire into two 6' (1.8 m) pieces and coil all of it around the 1mm mandrel.

2. On a 1' (30.5 cm) piece of 20g wire, make a mark at 1½" (3.8 cm). Leaving the tail, make a simple loop around the smallest section of the stepped forming pliers (or a 13mm mandrel). Center the loop at the top of the longer length of wire as you would on a wrapped loop.

3. Open the loop as if to open a jump ring and slide on a coil to fully encircle the loop. Trim the coil and slide off the excess. Wrap the shorter tail of 20g wire around the longer wire 3 times. Spiral in the tail toward the large loop. Hammer the spiral with the ball-peen hammer before it's completely tucked in. Trim the longer wire to ½" (1.3 cm).

4. Using the round-nose pliers where they are about 4mm thick, make a simple loop with the ½" (1.3 cm) wire to the back of the link.

5. Hammer the coiled loop with a rawhide or plastic mallet on a steel bench block to harden but not flatten it. Hammer the outside of the small loop to strengthen it.

6. Repeat Steps 2–5 to make a total of 8 links.

7. To join the links, open the loop as if to open a jump ring, loop it over the coiled part of another link, and close the loop.

8. With the 3" (7.5 cm) piece of 16g wire, hold the wire centered in the round-nose pliers in the same 4mm place in Step 4. Bring the 2 wires up toward each other, forming a U. Continue wrapping around until they extend out in opposite directions. Spiral the two ends in opposite directions and hammer if desired.

9. Attach the T bar made in Step 8 to the small loop on a link with a chain made of the 3 jump rings.

10. Dip the necklace in liver of sulfur solution if desired, then polish.

LEVEL 3

FINISHED SIZE: 8" (20.5 cm)

TECHNIQUES USED

Coiling (22), spiraling (22), simple loops (19), opening and closing jump rings (23), hammering (17), oxidizing (27)

materials

13' (4 m) of sterling silver 24-gauge dead-soft wire

3' (.9 m) of sterling silver 20-gauge dead-soft wire

3" (7.5 cm) of sterling silver 16-gauge dead-soft wire

3 sterling silver 4.5mm 18-gauge jump rings

tools

Chain-nose pliers
Round-nose pliers
Flat-nose pliers
Flush cutters
Large stepped forming pliers (or 13mm mandrel)
1mm mandrel
Nylon-jaw pliers
Ball-peen hammer
Rawhide mallet
Steel bench block
Liver of sulfur (optional)
Polishing cloth (optional)

resources

Wire: Beaducation.

Collector's Club Necklace

DESIGNED BY **Cindy Wimmer**

With a few twists, coils,
and spirals, you'll have a new
collection of wireworked links.
Combine heavy-gauge wire links with
your favorite set of lampworked beads
for a stunning piece of art jewelry!

1. Jump rings (3 sizes): Wind 3' (.9 m) of 16g wire into coils on the 5mm mandrel. Cut into forty 7mm OD jump rings. Wind 6" (15 cm) of 16g wire into coils on the 6½mm mandrel. Cut into six 9mm OD jump rings. Wind 8" (20.5 cm) of 16g wire into coils on the 8mm mandrel. Cut into six 10mm OD jump rings.

2. Lampworked links: Using 16g wire, create a simple loop on one end and then slide on a spacer, lampworked bead, and another spacer. Trim wire to ¾" (2 cm) and make a simple loop. Repeat for all of the lampworked beads. Attach two 10mm OD jump rings to each lampworked ring.

3. Small swirl link: Wind the 20g wire on the 2mm mandrel to create a coil. Cut a ⅞" (2.2 cm) length of coil. Cut a 4" (10 cm) length of 14g wire. Grasp one end of the wire with the back of the round-nose pliers and make a loop. Hold the loop with flat-nose pliers and form a loose spiral. Add the coil piece and press the coil ends down slightly with chain-nose pliers to secure. Trim the wire at the top of the spiral to ¾" (2 cm) and make a simple loop with the round-nose pliers. Repeat for a total of 3 small swirl links.

4. Double swirl link: Wind the 22g wire on the 2mm mandrel to create a coil. Cut a 1⅝" (4 cm) length of coil. Cut a 6" (15 cm) length of 14g wire. Create a small spiral at the end of the wire. Hold the spiral with the flat-nose pliers while shaping the wire into a circle about 17mm diameter. Hammer the small spiral. Slide on the coil piece and push it is snug against the spiral. Trim the coil if it is too long. Wrap the remaining wire around a 13mm mandrel, forming an S shape. Make a complete circle with the wire and trim the tail to ⅝" (1.5 cm) beyond the base of the circle. Create a small spiral on the end of the wire. Hammer the spiral and the left half of the circle. Repeat for 2 more double swirl links.

5. Rustic spring link: Cut 11½" (29 cm) of 14g wire. Wrap the wire loosely around a 6mm mandrel, wrapping the wire over itself a few times to create a "messy" look. Slide the coil off the mandrel. Insert the tip of the round-nose pliers between the last 2 coils to loosen and separate. Insert the edge of the flat-nose pliers between the first and second coil and bend the first coil up perpendicular to the rest of the coils. Repeat on the opposite end. Hold the end loops with pliers and twist so that the loops are on the same plane if necessary. Repeat for 3 more rustic spring links.

6. Attach the wire links to the lampworked links using the appropriate-sized jump rings. Use 2 jump rings to attach each link. You may find that the loops on some of the lampworked links need to be adjusted to connect properly; simply hold the loops with pliers and turn them perpendicular.

7. Dip the necklace in liver of sulfur solution and then buff with steel wool. Place in a rotary tumbler to work-harden and polish.

LEVEL 2 ●●

FINISHED SIZE: 33" (84 cm)

TECHNIQUES USED

Making jump rings (23), simple loops (19), spiraling (22), coiling (22), hammering (17), oxidizing (27)

materials

3½' (1 m) of sterling silver 14-gauge dead-soft wire

12' (3.7 m) of sterling silver 16-gauge dead-soft wire

3½' (1 m) of sterling silver 20-gauge half hard wire

6' (1.8 m) of sterling silver 22-gauge half-hard wire

22 sterling silver 5mm spacers

11 silvered ivory 10x14mm–11x31mm lampworked beads

3 silvered ivory 15mm lampworked rings

1 silvered ivory 24mm lampworked ring

tools

Round-nose pliers

Flat-nose pliers

Chain-nose pliers

Flush cutters

Ball-peen hammer

Steel bench block

2mm, 5mm, 6½mm, 8mm, and 13mm mandrels

Liver of sulfur

Fine steel wool, #0000

Rotary tumbler

resources

Lampworked beads: Kab's Creative Concepts.

The Tears That Never Fell Earrings

DESIGNED BY **Donna Spadafore**

Little drops of silver,
clinging to one another,
hoping to never fall.
Just a few simple elements combine
to make this original pair of earrings.

1 Cut each piece of wire in half. Use the torch to create balls on both ends of the 22g wire and the 26g wire. Ball one end of each 20g wire.

2 Measure 2" (5 cm) from the ball on one piece of 20g wire and cut. File the end smooth for the earring post. Measure ³⁄₈" (1 cm) from the un-balled end and create a 90° bend.

3 Holding the wire at the bend with the tip of the round-nose pliers, begin a spiral. Continue for 2 complete rounds.

4 At the end of the second complete round, bend the wire downward at a 90° angle to the spiral. Hammer this part of the earring, flattening the ball end first, then hammering just hard enough up the rest of the wire to harden it and flatten it a little. Hold the post against the side of the bench block and rotate it to get to the whole spiral. Be very careful; just tap it with the hammer to keep from creating marks on the back of the spiral with the edge of the bench block.

5 Shape one piece of 22g wire into a U with the ball ends almost touching. Make a slight bend outward about ¹⁄₈" (3 mm) below the ball on each side, then press the bent portions together until they almost meet. Hammer the wire to harden it and flatten the balled ends.

6 Position the 22g wire from Step 5 so that the U-shaped portion surrounds the flattened end of the 20g wire. The flattened ends of the 22g wire should straddle the 20g wire just above the end.

7 Gently flatten the ball ends of the 26g wire and cut it in half.

8 Using the 26g wire, bind the wires positioned in Step 6 together at the point where the 22g wire bends outward. When binding the wires, hold the flattened end of the 26g wire in front of the earring and begin wrapping. Wrap the 3 wires together 2–3 times, then wrap only the 20g wire with the 26g wire 4 times. Trim the 26g wire close to the 20g wire and press it close to the back of the 20g wire with bent-nose pliers.

9 Repeat Steps 2–8 for the second earring, making the spiral in Step 3 in the opposite direction from the first earring.

LEVEL 2 ● ●

FINISHED SIZE: 1" (2.5 cm)

TECHNIQUES USED
Balling (18), spiraling (22), hammering (17)

materials

5" (12.5 cm) of fine silver 20-gauge round wire

1³⁄₄" (4.5 cm) of fine silver 22-gauge round wire

4" (10 cm) of fine silver 26-gauge round wire

tools

Butane torch
Round-nose pliers
Flat-nose pliers
Bent-nose pliers
Hammer
Steel bench block
Metal file

resources

Wire: Metalliferous.

Lightning bolts for your ears!
Try any small bead to change
the look of this design,
or extend it longer, add a clasp,
and make a collar of stone and wire
for a striking choker.

Zigzag Earrings

DESIGNED BY **Denise Peck**

1. String 1 turquoise bead onto each head pin and trim the extending wire to ½" (1.3 cm).

2. Make a very small simple loop at the end of each head pin.

3. Attach 1 head pin to 1 ear wire. Attach a second head pin directly above the bead on first head pin, right above the bead. Attach 4 more in the same manner (above the bead of the previous head pin). Repeat for the second earring.

LEVEL 1 ●
FINISHED SIZE: 2 1/2" (6.5 cm)
TECHNIQUES USED
Simple loops (19)

materials

12 sterling silver 3/4" (2 cm) 26-gauge balled head pins
2 sterling silver ear wires
12 turquoise 5mm round beads

tools

Chain-nose pliers
Small round-nose pliers
Flush cutters

resources

Head pins: Fusion Beads. *Ear wires:* Artbeads.
Turquoise beads: Fire Mountain Gems.

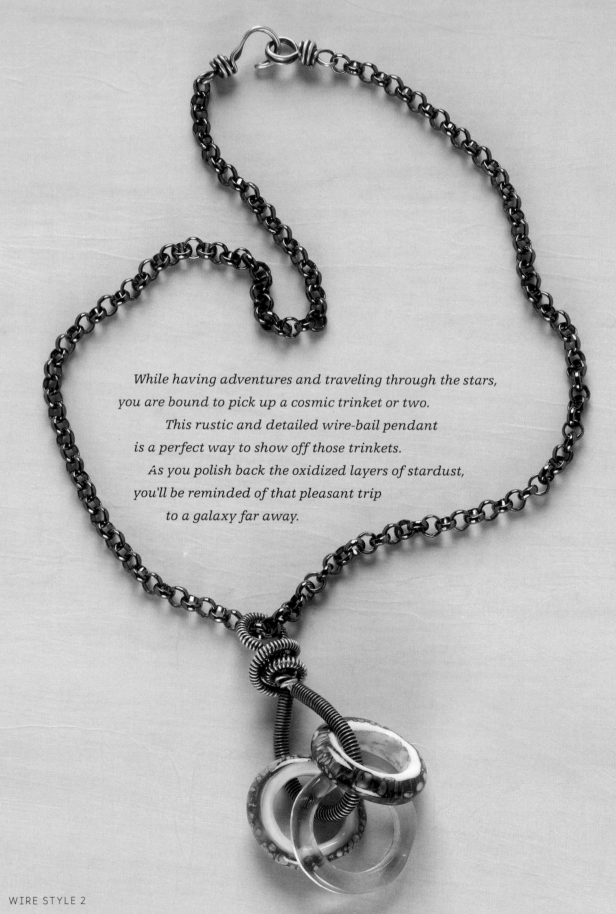

While having adventures and traveling through the stars,
you are bound to pick up a cosmic trinket or two.
This rustic and detailed wire-bail pendant
is a perfect way to show off those trinkets.
As you polish back the oxidized layers of stardust,
you'll be reminded of that pleasant trip
to a galaxy far away.

Cosmic Trinkets Necklace

DESIGNED BY **Kerry Bogert**

1. Coil the copper wire around the $\frac{1}{16}$" (2 mm) mandrel to make a 2½" (6.5 cm) wire coil. Trim excess wire and flush cut the ends of the coil. Remove from the mandrel.

2. Slide the coiled copper wire onto a 9" (23 cm) piece of 18g silver wire about 1½" (3.8 cm) from one end of the 18g wire. Form a U-shaped bend in the copper coil. Slide the 3 lampworked glass rings onto the bend in the wire.

3. Lock the lampworked glass rings onto the bent wire by wrapping the shorter end of the exposed silver core wire around the longer end as for a wrapped loop. Trim the excess shorter wire, but do not trim the longer length of silver wire.

4. With the 22g sterling wire, tightly wrap a 4" (10 cm) coil around the exposed 18g silver wire just above the wrapped area from Step 3. Trim the excess 22g wire; about 1½" (3.8 cm) of 18g wire should still be bare.

5. Treat the coiled area of 18g wire like a single piece of wire. With the back of the round-nose pliers, create a wrapped loop with a large hole that will act as the bail of the pendant. When closing the loop, wrap the coiled 18g wire over the wrapped wire from Step 3. Use the chain-nose pliers to tuck the excess bare wire inside the wrapping and trim any excess wire.

6. String the pendant on the length of rolo chain.

7. Cut the remaining 9" (23 cm) of 18g wire in half, making two 4½" (11.5 cm) pieces. With 1 piece, form a wrapped loop attached to the last link of the rolo chain. Wrap the tail 2 times around of the round nose pliers (about midway on the barrel) to make the eye of the hook-and-eye clasp, then wrap the loops closed over of the previous loop's wrapping.

8. With the remaining 18g wire, make a wrapped loop attached to the other end of the rolo chain as in Step 7. About 1" (2.5 cm) from the wrapping that closes the first loop, bend the wire back on itself. With chain-nose pliers, grasp the 2 parallel wires and wrap the tail over the wrapping of the starting loop. With round-nose pliers, bend the parallel wires into a hook.

9. Dip the pendant in liver of sulfur solution and then buff with steel wool. Place in a rotary tumbler to work-harden and polish.

LEVEL 2 ● ●

FINISHED SIZE: 18" (45.5 cm)

TECHNIQUES USED
Coiling (22), wrapped loops (20), simple hooks (24)

materials

18" (45.5 cm) of sterling silver 18-gauge dead-soft wire

3' (.9 m) of sterling silver 22-gauge dead-soft wire

2' (61 cm) of copper 22-gauge wire

3 lampworked 25mm glass rings

17" (43 cm) of gunmetal 4.3mm rolo chain

tools

Chain-nose pliers
Round-nose pliers
Flush cutters
$\frac{1}{16}$" (2 mm) mandrel
Liver of sulfur
Polishing cloth
Fine steel wool, #0000
Rotary tumbler

resources

Lampworked glass beads: Kab's Creative Concepts. *Gunmetal colored chain:* Rings & Things.

*Mixing metals is fun,
especially when there are no rules.
Add texture and pattern
to metal discs and washers,
and you'll have a jingly charm
bracelet in no time.*

Going in Circles Bracelet

DESIGNED BY **Cindy Wimmer**

① Coil the 18g wire 18 times around the 5mm mandrel. Cut the coils into 18 jump rings.

② Add texture and designs to each of the 18 metal discs and washers as follows: Using an awl and hammer, create dots. With a ball-peen hammer, add random indentations by varying the impact of the blow when hammering. Create lines with the back of a riveting hammer, crisscrossing them for different textured looks. Punch a hole in each of the discs and washers with the metal hole punch or awl.

③ Cut the 16g wire into six 4½" (11.5 cm) pieces. Hold the Sharpie on the center of the wire and bend the wire into a U shape. Cross each end of the wire over the Sharpie, pressing tightly against the mandrel to form a complete circle. Both wire ends should stick straight out perpendicular to the Sharpie. Remove from the Sharpie. Measure 1 wire tail ¾" (2 cm) from the center of the circle and trim. Make a simple loop. With chain-nose pliers, bend the second wire tail at the center of the circle so that it is perpendicular. Measure the second tail at ⅝" (1.5 cm) and trim. Make a simple loop that is perpendicular to the first. Repeat with the remaining 5 pieces.

④ Open the perpendicular simple loops and attach each one to the horizontal loop of another link, forming a chain.

⑤ Cut a 1⅜" (3.5 cm) piece of 16g wire. Create a figure-eight link, turning the loops perpendicular to each other with flat-nose pliers. Cut 3" (7.5 cm) of 16g wire and create a simple hook. Hammer the curve of the hook with the hammer and steel bench block. Attach the hook and the figure-eight link to opposite ends of the bracelet.

⑥ Attach the discs and washers to the bracelet using jump rings. Add 2 pieces to one side of each round link and 1 piece to the other side. Alternate for the 6 links of the bracelet.

⑦ Dip the necklace in liver of sulfur solution and then buff with steel wool. Place in a rotary tumbler to work-harden and polish.
Note: Oxidization may be uneven when copper and silver are oxidized together. In this case, remove the silver pieces and oxidize them separately. Brass does not darken in liver of sulfur, so to get the effect of oxidization, mark any stamped and indented areas with the black Sharpie marker.

LEVEL 3

FINISHED SIZE: 7½" (19 cm)

TECHNIQUES USED
Coiling (22), making jump rings (23), simple loops (19), figure-eight links (19), simple hooks (24), hammering (17)

materials
3' (.9 m) of copper 16-gauge wire
20" (51 cm) of copper 18-gauge wire
2 copper ¼" (6 mm) ID washers
2 copper ⅜" (1 cm) ID washers
2 copper 5/16" (8 mm) ID washers
2 sterling silver ⅝" (1.5 cm) discs
2 sterling silver ½" (1.3 cm) discs
2 sterling silver 5/16" (8 mm) washers
4 brass ⅝" (1.5 cm) discs
2 brass ½" (1.3 cm) discs

tools
Large round-nose pliers
Small round-nose pliers
Chain-nose pliers
Flat-nose pliers
Flush cutters
2mm and 5mm steel mandrel
Metal hole-punch pliers (or an awl)
Ball-peen hammer
Riveting hammer
Various objects to add texture to the metal (letter I stamp, awl, design stamps, etc.)
Steel bench block
Black fine-tip Sharpie marker
Liver of sulfur
Fine steel wool, #0000 (optional)
Polishing cloth
Rotary tumbler

resources
Copper washers and metal hole-punch pliers: Fundametals. *Sterling silver and brass discs:* Bopper.

In some societies, the circle
is a symbol of the feminine spirit.
This pin symbolizes the connection
women have with one another.
The pin is best suited to be worn
with a loosely woven coat, jacket, or sweater.

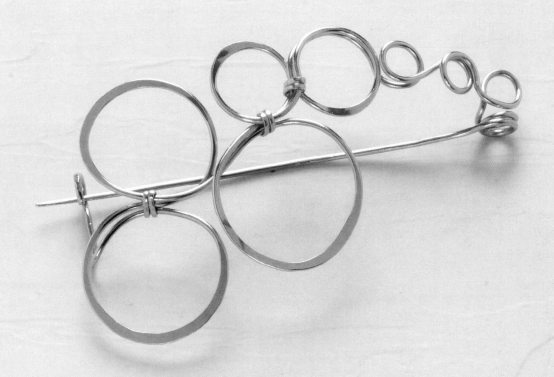

La Femme Brooch

DESIGNED BY **Connie Fox**

1 Cut 2" (5 cm) of 16g wire and set aside. Starting 2" (5 cm) from one end of the remaining 16g wire, begin wrapping circles. Bring the long end of the wire fully around the ¾" jaw of the stepped forming pliers or mandrel. Remove the mandrel and place it right next to the first circle. Wrap the wire in the opposite direction fully around the mandrel again. Remove the mandrel. Make a third circle next to the first two.

2 Continuing along the wire in the same direction as in Step 1, use the smaller mandrel or jaw to make two additional circles. Use round-nose pliers to make three small circles.

3 On the steel bench block, flatten all the circles with the ball-peen hammer. Pull the circles far enough apart to avoid hammering wire on top of wire. Use the gold-plated wire to join the circles together, wrapping twice around the circles where they touch.

4 Make a counterclockwise coil next to and perpendicular to the last circle by wrapping twice around the round-nose pliers. Place the long round-nose pliers into the double coil and bend the pin stem toward the pin. Leave enough space between the pin stem and the pin to hold clothing, about ⅜–½" (10–13 mm).

5 Bend the short end of the wire up to the pin stem. Use round-nose pliers to curve the end around the pin and form a hook. Trim any excess and file smooth.

6 Trim the pin stem so that it extends ¼" (6 mm) beyond the clasp. Reopen the pin stem. Taper the end of the pin with the file. Harden and straighten the pin stem using the nylon mallet on the bench block. Smooth the pin stem with abrasive paper followed by fine steel wool. Use long round-nose pliers to reset the pin stem into proper position.

LEVEL 3 ● ● ●

FINISHED SIZE: 3¾" (9.5 cm)

TECHNIQUES USED
Coiling (22), hammering (17)

materials
3' (.9 m) of nickel-silver 16-gauge round wire
6" (15 cm) of gold-plated 18-gauge dead-soft half-round wire

tools
Flush cutters
Long round-nose pliers
Chain-nose pliers
Large stepped forming pliers or ¾" and ½" mandrels
Ball-peen hammer
Nylon mallet
Steel bench block
Flat needle file
6" (15 cm) flat file
#600 abrasive paper
Fine steel wool, #0000

resources
All materials: Jatayu.

Create a more asymmetrical look
for this bracelet design
by alternating different beads
within the oval wire sections.
Change the width of the bracelet
by adding or subtracting metal tube beads
as a design alternative.

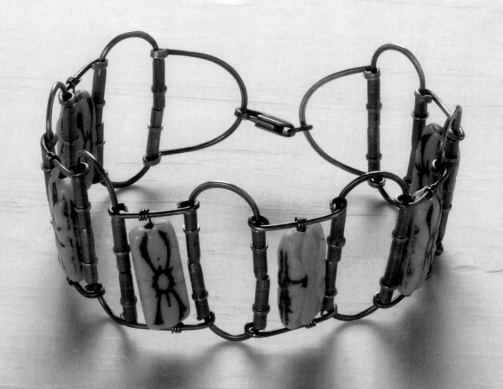

Wire Cuff

DESIGNED BY **Lorelei Eurto**

1. Cut two 1½" (3.8 cm) pieces of 20g wire. Curve each piece around the large Sharpie, forming a U shape. Form parallel simple loops on both ends of both U shapes. Hammer the curves flat. Attach the lobster clasp to one U with the 4mm jump ring.

2. Cut twelve ¾" (2 cm) pieces of 20g wire. Hammer all the ends flat. With round-nose pliers, make a small loop on all the ends, all going in the same direction. These are the link connectors.

3. Cut seven 3" (7.5 cm) pieces of 20g wire. Mark each piece ¾" (2 cm) from one end. Place the mark against the ballpoint pen and bend the wire around to create a U shape with one long end and one short end. String 2 brass tube beads onto the long end. At the end of the tube beads, curve the wire around the pen again so that the long end meets the short end of the U, forming an oval shape. Pulling the two wire ends apart, string 2 more brass tube beads so that the wire ends meet inside one of the tube beads. Repeat this step 6 more times, creating 7 oval links. Hammer each curve, being careful not to hammer the tube beads.

4. To join the links together, open the loops on the link connectors and attach one loop to each oval link at the outsides of the brass tube beads. Close the loops with flat-nose pliers. This creates rectangular sections that will hold the pressed-glass beads.

5. Cut six 2" (5 cm) pieces of 22g wire. Coil a piece of 22g wire around the center of 1 link connector tightly 3 times. String 1 pressed-glass rectangle bead. Wrap the remaining wire around the center of the link connector on the other end. Trim any excess wire with the flush cutters on the back of the bracelet. Repeat 5 more times with the remaining glass beads and wire.

6. Attach the curved ends made in Step 1 by opening the loops and attaching them to the end oval links at the outsides of the brass tubes.

LEVEL 2 ● ●

FINISHED SIZE: 7³/4" (19.5 cm)

TECHNIQUES USED
Simple loops (19), hammering (17), opening and closing jump rings (23), flush cutting (17), coiling (22)

materials

30" (76 cm) of oxidized brass 20-gauge wire

6 aqua 8x20mm pressed-glass rectangle beads

28 brass 10mm tube beads

1 brass 4mm jump ring

1 brass 5x10mm lobster clasp

9" (23 cm) of brass 24-gauge artist wire

tools

Round-nose pliers

Flat-nose pliers

Flush cutters

Ball-peen hammer

Steel bench block

Large Sharpie marker

Ballpoint pen

resources

Brass wire: Patina Queen. *Glass beads*: EmMi Beads. *Brass tubes*: Hands of the Hills. *Brass lobster clasp and jump rings*: Vintaj Brass Co.

The versatility of lariats abounds.
    This extra-long design can be worn
    multiple ways for lots of different looks.
        The frosty blue and minty green palette
is a classic color combination making
    for a true, no-fail, must-have piece.

Coloring an Opera Lariat

DESIGNED BY **Kerry Bogert**

1 Coil a 6' (1.8 m) piece of turquoise-colored wire around an 8" (20.5 cm) piece of 16g silver wire for 6" (15 cm). Flush cut the end of 20g wire.

2 Wrap the entire coil-covered 16g wire around a ½" mandrel. Remove the coil from the mandrel and use wire cutters to cut it into 2 individual rings, treating them as making jump rings. Use chain-nose pliers to bring the ring ends together and close the loop. Repeat for each ring.

3 Repeat Steps 1 and 2 with a 2' (61 cm) piece of green-colored wire and 3" (7.5 cm) piece of 16g silver wire to create a single green coiled ring.

4 Use an 8" (20.5 cm) piece of 18g silver wire to create a spiral head pin as follows: form a 90° bend in the wire about 2" (5 cm) from one end. Grasp the shorter side of the wire with tip of the round-nose pliers next to the bend. Using your dominant hand, begin a spiral around the tip of the pliers, then continue to spiral from the center out, making 2 complete turns. Use wire cutters to trim the spiral.

5 String 1 hollow glass bead, 1 blue coiled ring, and 1 hollow glass bead onto the spiral head pin. Lock beads in place by using round-nose pliers to make a large wrapped loop with the remaining wire. Wrap over the initial wrapping to create a chunky wrap. Trim excess wire. Open one of the coiled blue wire rings with chain-nose pliers and attach it to the wrapped loop of the hollow bead pendant. Close the loop. Set aside.

6 With a 6" (15 cm) piece of 18g green-colored wire, form a wrapped loop. Before closing the loop, add one of the lampworked glass rings. Form a second wrapped loop and wrap excess wire over the pervious wrapping. Trim excess wrapped wire.

7 With a 6" (15 cm) piece of 18g green-colored wire, begin to form another wrapped loop. Before closing the loop, connect it to the loop created in Step 6. Trim excess wire. String 1 lampworked glass round bead, 1 coiled wire ring, and 1 lampworked glass round. Form another wrapped loop, locking the beads in place.

8 Use the colored wire jump rings to attach a pendant to each ends of the rolo chain.

LEVEL 2

FINISHED SIZE: 53½" (136 cm)

TECHNIQUES USED
Coiling (22), spiraling (22), wrapped loops (20)

materials

14" (35.5 cm) of sterling silver 16-gauge wire
8" (20.5 cm) of sterling silver 18-gauge wire
4' (1.2 m) turquoise-colored copper 20-gauge wire
2' (61 m) of green-colored copper 18-gauge wire
4' (1.2 m) of sterling silver 3.6mm rolo chain
1 blue 25mm lampworked glass hollow bead
1 green 20mm lampworked glass hollow bead
1 blue and green 20mm lampworked glass ring bead
2 blue 15mm lampworked glass round bead
2 blue-colored wire 6mm jump rings

tools

Chain-nose pliers
Round-nose pliers
Flush cutters
½" mandrel

resources

Colored wire: Paramount Wire Co.
Lampworked beads: Kab's Creative Concepts.
Colored jump rings: Blue Buddha Boutique.

A beautiful bail and matching links
come together easily with copper wire.
Try these easy-to-make swirls
in sterling or brass wire
to go with any set of beads.

Caramel Swirl Necklace

DESIGNED BY **Cindy Wimmer**

1 Wind the 22g wire onto the 2mm steel mandrel to create a coil 1⅞" (5 cm) long. Set aside.

2 Coiled focal: Using the tip of the small round-nose pliers, grasp the end of the 16g wire and make a loop. Hold the loop with the flat-nose pliers and create a 1½-turn spiral with the wire. Hold the spiral with the flat-nose pliers and use your fingers to guide and bend the wire into an 18mm circle. Hammer the inner spiral to flatten.

3 Slide the coil onto the circle. Measuring from the top center of the spiral, trim the tail wire to ⅞" (2.2 cm). With the fattest part of the jaw of round-nose pliers, make a simple loop. Hammer the loop to flatten.

4 Make a small simple loop on one end of 2" (5 cm) of 20g wire to make an eye pin and string a lampworked focal bead. Attach to the simple loop on the coiled focal with a wrapped loop.

5 Spiral links: Cut eight 5" (12.5 cm) pieces of 18g wire. Repeat Step 2 to create 8 links, but making a smaller 13mm circle.

6 Use flat-nose pliers to bend the tail wires up 90° (perpendicular to the spirals). Trim the tail wires to ½" (1.3 cm). Make simple loops with round-nose pliers, then center the loops. Hammer to flatten the links.

7 To assemble the necklace, attach lampworked beads to the coiled focal using 3" (7.5 cm) of 20g wire. Attach the other side of the 3" length of wire to a spiral link with a wrapped loop. Continue alternating wire-wrapped lampworked beads with coiled links.

8 Cut 2" (5 cm) of 18g wire to create a figure-eight link. Use the flat-nose pliers to turn the loops perpendicular. Repeat to make a second link and attach one to each end of the necklace.

9 Cut a 6" (15 cm) piece of 18g wire. Create a spiral link as in Step 2, this time with the circle 14mm in diameter. From the top center of the spiral, use the flat-nose pliers to bend the wire up 90°. Measure the wire ¼" (6 mm) from the spiral and bend the wire over the back of the large round-nose pliers to create a hook. Trim the wire so that the end is lined up flush with the edge of the circle. Make a simple loop with the tips of the small round-nose pliers. Hammer the circle and the curve of the hook to flatten.

10 Dip the necklace in liver of sulfur solution and then buff with steel wool if desired. Place in a rotary tumbler to work-harden and polish.

LEVEL 3

FINISHED SIZE: 17½" (44.5 cm)

TECHNIQUES USED
Coiling (22), spiraling (22), simple loops (19), figure-eight links (19), simple hooks (24), oxidizing (27)

materials
6" (12.5 cm) of copper 16-gauge wire
4' (1.2 m) of copper 18-gauge wire
2½' (76 cm) of copper 20-gauge wire
2' (61 cm) of copper 22-gauge wire
9 lampworked glass 14x19mm beads

tools
Large round-nose pliers
Small round-nose pliers
Chain-nose pliers
Flat-nose pliers
Flush cutters
2mm steel mandrel
Ball-peen hammer
Steel bench block
Black Sharpie marker
Liver of sulfur
Fine steel wool, #0000 (optional)
Polishing cloth
Rotary tumbler

resources
Lampworked beads: Kim Typanski.

Garden Heart Bracelet

DESIGNED BY **Jodi Bombardier**

*Although not true filigree, this bracelet evokes
that style and can open the door
to lots of design possibilities.
Try it with your favorite gemstones.*

LEVEL 3 ● ● ●

FINISHED SIZE: 7" (18 cm)

TECHNIQUES USED
Straightening wire (17), flush cutting (17),
simple loops (19), coiling (22), wrapped
loops (20)

materials

8" (20.5 cm) of sterling silver 16-gauge dead-soft square wire

6-7' (1.8-2.1 m) of sterling silver 26-gauge dead-soft round wire

3 green amethyst 8mm faceted beads

10-14 mystic topaz 3mm beads

4-6 sterling silver 2mm Thai cornerless cube beads

6 sterling silver 3mm daisy spacers

1' (30.5 cm) of sterling silver chain

2 sterling silver 6mm 18-gauge jump rings

1 sterling silver toggle clasp

tools

Flush cutters

Chain-nose pliers

Round-nose pliers

Wire-straightening pliers

Ruler

Black Sharpie marker

Low-stick tape

resources

Semiprecious stones: TAJ Company. *Sterling silver wire:* Indian Jewelers Supply. *Sterling silver chain:* SII Findings. *Jump rings:* Rio Grande. *Thai beads:* Ands Silver. *Clasp:* Tierra Cast.

1. Straighten and flush cut four 2" (5 cm) pieces of 16g wire for the frame wire.

2. With round-nose pliers, make a small loop at the end of the wire, then continue to loop around another ¼ turn to begin the scroll. To avoid twisting the wire, make a quarter of the loop, turn the pliers and insert them into the loop from the opposite side, then finish making the loop.

3. Repeat Step 2 on the other end of the wire with the loop going in the opposite direction. Set aside.

4. Repeat Steps 2–3 on the remaining three 2" (5 cm) pieces of 16g wire, using the completed piece as a template; the remaining pieces need to be the same size or as close as possible.

5. Place 2 frame wires on a flat surface, positioned with 2 loops facing each other to form the top of the heart and 2 loops back-to-back to form the bottom of the heart. With a Sharpie, mark both frame wires at the bottom of the heart just above where the 2 wires touch.

6. Cut 18" (45.5 cm) of 26g wire. Coil one of the frame wires from the mark to halfway inside the top loop. Cut the beginning wire tail but do not cut the ending wire tail.

7. Repeat Steps 5–6 for the other set of frame wires.

8. Cut 12" (30.5 cm) of 26g wire. With one of the uncoiled frame wires, coil from halfway inside of the top loop to just outside of the top loop.

9. Slide either a mystic topaz bead or a Thai bead onto the 26g wire, then coil the frame wire 2–4 times.

10. Repeat Step 9, adding topaz and Thai beads randomly and coiling up to the Sharpie mark made in Step 5. Cut the beginning wire tail, but do not cut the ending wire tail.

11. Tape the top of 2 frame wires together. With the wire tail from Step 10, coil the bottom 2 frame wires together. Add more beads to the frame wire and continue coiling to just outside of the bottom loops. Cut the wire tail and remove the tape.

12. Repeat Steps 8–11 for the second set of frame wires.

13. Cut 6" (15 cm) of 26g wire and coil the 2 top loops of the heart frame wires together 4–6 times. Cut the wire tails. Repeat on the second heart frame wires.

14. With one of the wire tails from Step 6, string 1 daisy spacer, 1 green amethyst bead, and 1 daisy spacer.

15. Thread the other wire tail from Step 7 through the 3 beads so the wires crisscross and the beads are in the center of the 2 heart frames. Pull the 2 wire tails so the beads are against the frame wires. Coil both tail wires 3 times around the loops opposite the spacer beads. Cut both wire tails.

16. Cut 8" (20.5 cm) of 26g wire. Fold the wire in half and loop the center of the wire around the base of the 2 bottom heart loops where the frames connect. Slide on 1 daisy spacer, one 8mm green amethyst bead, and 1 daisy spacer onto both wires. With the beads flush against the bottom of the heart frame, coil 1 wire around the other wire 3–4 times and cut, leaving the other wire tail.

17. Cut six 1¾" (4.5 cm) pieces of chain. Make a wrapped loop on one 26g wire tail, but before closing it, slide 3 pieces of chain onto the loop. Wrap the loop closed and cut the wire tail. Repeat on the other side of the bracelet.

18. Attach the toggle with a jump ring on each end of the bracelet. Remove some chain links if the bracelet is too large.

When you want to show off
a one-of-a-kind focal, no ordinary bail will do.
Use three different gauges of wire
to create a bail and links
that will complement handmade art beads.

Fallen to Earth Necklace

DESIGNED BY **Cindy Wimmer**

1. Coil the 20g wire around a 14g mandrel until the coil is 7" (18 cm) long. Cut a piece of coil half as long as the radius of the donut focal, about ⅞" (2.2 cm). Cut the remaining coil into eight ⅝" (1.5 cm) pieces and set aside.

2. Cut 4½" (11.5 cm) of 16g wire. Make a simple loop on one end in the back of the large round-nose pliers. String the ⅞" (2.2 cm) piece of coiled wire and insert into the center of the donut bead. Bend the wire in a U shape to create a bail, then remove it and set aside.

3. Cut eight 2½" (6.5 cm) pieces of 16g wire. With 2 of the pieces, make a simple loop on the back of the large round-nose pliers. With the remaining pieces, make a simple loop on the back of the small round-nose pliers. Add a ⅝" (1.5 cm) coil to each and finish with a smaller simple loop.

4. Cut eight 6" (15 cm) of 18g wire and randomly wrap one over each of the coiled wire links and the bail. Cut an 8" (20.5 cm) piece of 18g wire and randomly wrap over the coil on the bail. Trim excess wire and press ends down.

5. Cut six 2½" (6.5 cm) pieces of 16g wire for eye pins.

6. Use 4" (10 cm) of 16g wire to make a simple hook. Hammer the curve flat.

7. Dip all wire pieces including the hook in liver of sulfur solution and then buff with steel wool. Place in a rotary tumbler for an hour to work-harden and polish.

8. Add the donut pendant to the bail. Press the back of the wire against the donut and create a simple loop at the end. Line up the loops so that the front loop is directly in front of the back loop.

9. Create eye pins by making a simple loop on one end of each of the 2½" (6.5 cm) wire pieces to hold the round beads. Add a round bead to each and finish with a simple loop.

10. Assemble the necklace by attaching the 2 coiled links with the larger simple loops to the bail first. Alternate wire links with bead links and finish one side by attaching the hook.

LEVEL 2 ● ●

FINISHED SIZE: 16 ¼" (41.5 cm)

TECHNIQUES USED
Coiling (22), simple loops (19), oxidizing (27), simple hooks (24), hammering (17)

materials
4' (1.2 m) of pure copper 16-gauge wire
4 ½' (1.4 m) of pure copper 18-gauge wire
5' (1.5 m) of pure copper 20-gauge wire
6 round 16mm polymer clay beads
1 polymer clay 2" (5 cm) donut bead

tools
Large round-nose pliers
Small round-nose pliers
Chain-nose pliers
Flat-nose pliers
Flush cutters
Ball-peen hammer
Steel bench block
Mandrel (a piece of 14-gauge wire, a 3/32 lampworked mandrel, or a 1/16 lampworked mandrel)
Liver of sulfur (optional)
Fine steel wool, #0000 (optional)
Rotary tumbler

resources
Polymer clay beads: Stories They Tell.

Tapered Spiked Earrings

DESIGNED BY **Lisa Niven Kelly**

*Use classic Egyptian coil links
in descending size
for these sassy earrings.
The surprise comes from
the tiny wired-on crystals
in the center of each spiral.*

1. Cut a 7" (18 cm), a 5" (12.5 cm), and a 3½" (9 cm) piece of 20g wire. Holding the wire in the back of the round-nose pliers (about 4mm diameter), bend each piece of wire into a U shape. Spiral each end out to the side, making the inside loops very small (1–2mm). Spiral each end of the 7" (18 cm) piece until it measures ⅞" (2.2 cm) across. Spiral the 5" (12.5 cm) piece until it measures ¾" (2 cm) across. Spiral the 3½" (9 cm) piece until it measures ⅝" (1.5 cm) across.

2. Push the 2 spirals on each piece together. Bend the pinched part of each link in the chain-nose pliers by placing the spirals within the jaws so that the tips of the spiral are just hiding within the top jaws of the pliers. Push slightly to start a bend. Place each so the mandrel fits snugly in the crease of that bend. The top of the spirals should line up with the center of the thickness of that mandrel. Continue that bend by bracing the spirals with your thumbs and pushing the top over with your index finger. The bottom loop of the U should be almost flush with the bottom of the spirals, and the bend in the top 2 wires should be flush with the tops of the spirals. Pinch in the top 2 wires so they touch.

3. To join these links, take the largest link in your left hand, holding it upside-down with the U pointing to the right. Hold the medium link in your right hand with the right side facing you and the U pointing down. Tuck the tip of the U in your right hand under the 2 wires on the U of the bottom link and up through the center of the two. Attach the medium link to the large, then join the small link to the medium.

4. Cut six 2" (5 cm) pieces of 24g wire. Make a tiny simple loop at one end of a 2" (5 cm) length of wire. String 1 bicone and 1 star spacer. Pass through the center of the largest spiral from front to back, then bring the wire across the back and out of the center of the opposing spiral. String 1 star spacer and 1 bicone and form another tiny simple loop as close to the bicone as possible. Trim any excess wire. Repeat for each of the 5 other links.

5. Cut two 3" (7.5 cm) lengths of 24g wire. Create a small spiral at one end of 1 piece of wire. String 1 bicone and 1 star spacer. Attach to the U shape on the smallest spiral link with a wrapped loop. Repeat with the other piece of wire to create a dangle on the other earring.

6. Open 1 jump ring and pass it under both top bent wires on 1 large spiral link. Attach an ear wire and close the jump ring. Repeat for the second earring.

7. Dip all the pieces in liver of sulfur solution, then polish.

LEVEL 3 ● ● ●

FINISHED SIZE: 1³/₄" (4.5 cm)

TECHNIQUES USED
Spiraling (22), oxidizing (27), wrapped loops (20), simple loops (19), opening and closing jump rings (23)

materials
3' (.9 m) of sterling silver 20-gauge dead-soft wire
1½' (45.5 cm) of sterling silver 24-gauge dead-soft wire
14 silver 4mm star spacers
14 blue zircon 3mm bicone crystals
2 silver 6mm jump rings
2 French ear wires

tools
Chain-nose pliers
Round-nose pliers
Flush cutters
Liver of sulfur
1mm mandrel
Polishing cloth

resources
All materials: Beaducation.

resources

A Silver Planet
310 5th Ave., 7th Fl.
New York, NY 10001
(917) 256-0296
asilverplanet.com

Ace Hardware
acehardwareoutlet.com

AD Adornments
adadornments.com

Ands Silver
(323) 254-5250
andssilver.com

Artbeads
11901 137th Ave. Ct. KPN
Gig Harbor, WA 98329
(866) 715-2323
artbeads.com

Bead Empire
1032 Sixth Ave.
New York, NY 10018
(212) 768-8818

Beads of Passion
beadsofpassion.etsy.com

Beaducation
1347 Laurel St.
San Carlos, CA 94070
(650) 654-7791
beaducation.com

Bello Modo
(360) 357-3443
bellomodo.com

Blue Buddha Boutique
4533 North Kedzie
Chicago, IL 60625
(866) 602-7464
bluebuddhaboutique.com

Boobie Beads
boobiebeads.etsy.com

Bopper
bopper.etsy.com

Chinook Jewelry
PO Box 420232
San Diego, CA 92142
chinookjewelry.com

E&E Bungalow
eandebungalow.etsy.com

Elaine Ray
elaineray.com
ornamentea.com

EmMi Beads
No. 4 West Park Row
Clinton, NY 13323
(315) 853-8760
emmibeads.com

Etsy
etsy.com

Every Heart Crafts
everyheartcrafts.com

Fire Mountain Gems
(800) 355-2137
firemountaingems.com

Fundametals
fundametals.net

Fusion Beads
3830 Stone Wy. N.
Seattle, WA 98103
(206) 782-4595
fusionbeads.com

Gardanne Glass
gardannebeads.etsy.com

Green Girl Studios
PO Box 19389
Asheville, NC 28815
greengirlstudios.com

Hands of the Hills
3016 78th Ave. SE
Mercer Island, WA 98040
(206) 232-4588
hohbead.com

Heather Wynn
heatherwynn.com
swoondimples.etsy.com

Humblebeads
humblebeads.etsy.com

Indian Jewelers Supply
2105 San Mateo NE
Albuquerque, NM 87111
(800) 545-6540
ijsinc.com

Jatayu
Connie Fox
(888) 350-6481
jatayu.com

Jena Fulcher
jenagirlbeads.com

Jewelry Supply
(866) 380-7464
jewelrysupply.com

Joan Miller Porcelain Beads
joanmiller.com

Kab's Creative Concepts
Kerry Bogert
991 Maple Dr.
Webster, NY 14580
(585) 944-0141
kabsconcepts.com

Keith O'Connor
keithraku@msn.com

Kelley's Beads
kelleysbeads.etsy.com

Kim Typanski
kim@typanski.com
nightingalegallery.com

Lynn Davis
expeditiond.etsy.com

Melek Karacan
horizonlap@hotmail.com

Metalliferous
34 West 46th St.
New York, NY 10036
(212) 944-0909
metalliferous.com

Moon Stumpp
(317) 525-2100
mixedmediajewelry.com
mixedmediajewelry.etsy.com

The Mykonos
245 Main St.
Hyannis, MA 02601
(888) 695-6667
mykonosbeads.com

Original Findings
originalfindings.etsy.com

Ornamentea
509 North West St.
Raleigh, NC 27603
(919) 834-6260
ornamentea.com

Paramount Wire Co.
2-8 Central Ave.
East Orange, NJ 07018
(973) 672-0500
parawire.com

Patina Queen
patinaqueen.com
patinaqueen.etsy.com

Rings & Things
304 East Second Ave.
Spokane, WA 99202
(800) 366-2156
rings-things.com

Rio Grande
(800) 545-6566
riogrande.com

Sears
(800) 697-3277
sears.com

SII Findings
(866) 434-6346
siifindings.com

Silk Road Treasures
28401 Ballard Dr., Unit F
Lake Forest, IL 60045
(866) 775-7710
silkroadtreasures.com

Stones Studios Too
stonestudiostoo.etsy.com

Stories They Tell
Christine Damm
storiestheytell.etsy.com

Studio Rent
studiorent.etsy.com

TAJ Company
42 West 48th St.
14th Fl.
New York, NY 10036
(800) 325-0825
tajcompany.com

Thunderbird Supply
2311 Vassar NE
Albuquerque, NM 87107
(505) 884-7770
thunderbirdsupply.com

Tierra Cast
3177 Guerneville Rd.
Santa Rosa, CA 95401
(800) 222-9939
tierracast.com

Vintaj Brass Co. (wholesale only)
vintaj.com

Walter's Beads
waltersbeads.etsy.com
York Beads
10 West 37th St.
New York, NY 10018
(800) 223-6676
yorkbeads.com

You and Me Findings
9087 Las Tunas Dr.
Temple City, CA 91780
(866) 286-2622
youandmefindings.net

Zoa Art
zoaart.etsy.com

contributors

Kerry Bogert

Kerry Bogert is a mom, author, artist, and designer living in western New York with her husband and three kids. When she isn't making her own glass beads, she is coming up with new ways to show off lampwork in colorful, creative jewelry. Look for her book, *Totally Twisted* (Interweave), and see more of her work at kabsconcepts.com.

Jodi Bombardier

Jodi Bombardier is a self-taught jewelry designer who discovered wire wrapping in 2005 and knew that she had found her niche. Her jewelry is currently sold in stores in Arizona and Utah. She is the author of *Weave, Wrap, Coil* (Interweave). More of her jewelry designs are available on her site, Jewels-By-Jules.com. Find helpful hints, tips, tutorials, and her blog at Online-Wire-Wrapping-Instructions .com. Jodi can be reached at Jodi@ Jewels-By-Jules.com.

Jane Dickerson

Jane Dickerson of Dickerson Ink is a freelance editor, writer, and jewelry designer. She was formerly the editor of *Step by Step Beads, Creative Jewelry,* and *Bead Star* magazines. Her jewelry designs have appeared in several books and magazines. Jane is the author of *Chain Style* (Interweave) and is coauthor of *Handcrafted Wire Findings* (Interweave).

Lorelei Eurto

Inspiration is never more than a foot away, as Lorelei Eurto works full time in an art museum in upstate New York. A self-taught jewelry designer, she has been creating handmade beaded and wire jewelry since 2007. Inspired by nature, texture, shapes, and color, Lorelei enjoys using artisan-made jewelry components in each of her designs. See more of Lorelei's jewelry at Lorelei1141.etsy.com and read more about her process at her blog, Lorelei1141.blogspot.com.

Connie Fox

Connie Fox has been making metal jewelry since 1997 and teaching since 2001. Her classes focus on large-scale wirework, cold connections, metal fabrication, jewelry design, and enameling. She is an adjunct professor with San Diego Community College Continuing Education and teaches Beginning Fabrication skills. Connie is the author of numerous jewelry-making articles and is a contributing editor to *Step by Step Wire Jewelry* magazine. She can be reached at Jatayu.com.

Lisa Niven Kelly

Lisa Niven Kelly finds joy in all things bead. She has been teaching beadwork and wirework since 1995. Her current work focuses on wirework, into which she incorporates beads whenever possible. When not teaching nationally, Lisa is home managing her online tool, kit, and supply shop (which now offers online classes), beaducation.com. She is the author of *Stamped Metal Jewelry* (Interweave).

Denise Peck

Denise Peck is the editor in chief of *Step by Step Wire Jewelry* magazine and author of *Wire Style* and *101 Wire Earrings*. She is coauthor of *Handcrafted Wire Findings* (Interweave). Denise went to jewelry-making school in New York City in 1999 to get her bench jeweler's certificate and joined *Lapidary Journal* in 2004. Her three instructional DVDs on Viking Knit, Fusing, and Wire Bezels are available at interweavestore.com. She can be contacted at dpeck@interweave .com.

Donna Spadafore

Donna Spadafore began making jewelry as a teenager. Starting out with seed beads and Nymo thread, she created beautiful beadwork sold throughout Ohio at powwows, craft fairs, and various other venues. She now works mostly with wire and gemstones to create her own original designs. See more of her work at gailavira.com.

Cindy Wimmer

Cindy Wimmer lives in Virginia with her husband, four sons, and their Shih Tzu. Her wire jewelry has been published in both national and international jewelry design publications. Cindy is the co-founder of ArtBLISS, hosting jewelry and mixed-media workshops in the Washington, D.C., area. Visit Cindy's website at sweetbeadstudio.com.

index

get caught up in these other creative and inspirational contemporary wire jewelry resources from Interweave

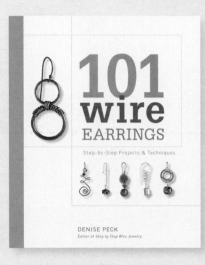

Weave, Wrap, Coil
Creating Artisan Wire Jewelry

Jodi Bombardier

ISBN 978-1-59668-200-9
$22.95

101 Wire Earrings
Step-by-Step Projects
and Techniques

Denise Peck

ISBN 978-1-59668-141-5
$19.95

Wire Style
50 Unique Jewelry Designs

Denise Peck

ISBN 978-1-59668-070-8
$19.95

Jewelry Making Daily

Join JewelryMakingDaily.com, an online community that shares your passion for jewelry. You'll get a free e-newsletter, free projects, a daily blog, a pattern store, galleries, artist interviews, contests, tips and techniques, and more. Sign up for *Jewelry Making Daily* at jewelrymakingdaily.com.

Check out *Jewelry Artist,* a trusted guide to the art of gems, jewelry making, design, beads, minerals, and more. From beginners to experienced artisans and businesses, *Jewelry Artist* can take you to a whole new level. Sign up for a subscription and look for all the issues at jewelryartistmagazine.com.

INTERWEAVE.
interweave.com